# VO__
# ROMANA

*or*

## *The Romans had a Word for it*

## John Parker

**Cressar Publications, Ludgvan, Penzance TR20 8XG**

# VOX ROMANA

Copyright © John H. D. Parker 2015

The right of John Parker to be identified as the author of this work has been asserted in accordance with sections 77 and 78 of the Copyright, Designs and Patents Act 1988.

Cressar Publications,
Ludgvan,
Penzance, Cornwall
TR20 8XG
UK

Printed and bound in Great Britain by Book Printing UK

ISBN 978-0-9535399-3-2

Distributed by York Publishing Services, 64 Hallfield Road, Layerthorpe, York. YO31 7ZQ

## Disclaimer

Every effort has been made to attribute the quotations in this collection to the correct source. Should there be any omissions or errors in this respect we apologise and shall be pleased to make the appropriate acknowledgements in any future editions.

# VOX ROMANA

*or The Romans had a Word for it*

English writers still come up with a number of Latin phrases in their work, and some of these are used widely in everyday speech. We talk about something being "in situ", or being interesting "per se", and some of us witter on "ad nauseam" and "ad infinitum" to our friends about our holiday experiences until we each become "persona non grata"; or we offer our children such advice as "carpe diem", even though they may regard us as being "non compos mentis". It was not only the Greeks who had a word for it: so did the Romans.

It seems to me that we don't always look closely enough at these useful phrases or link them firmly enough with happenings in our everyday lives (or even in the everyday lives of the Romans themselves). This little book seeks to take Latin phrases, ranging from the well-known to the obscure, and tie them up with familiar situations, giving us perhaps something to mutter under our breath even if we don't care to breathe our sentiments out loud.

The book also includes examples of how Latin has been and still is used, when appropriate, by writers in English. For anyone interested, or for anyone who thinks I may have made up more than one or two of the Latin phrases myself, and rather than overload the commentary text, I have listed any known or relevant sources in Appendix III (page 115).

Six of the illustrations are by Hannah Mitchell.

*By the same author*

Crossnumbers
Reading Latin Epitaphs
The Platonic Solids
Ad Hoc, Ad Lib, Ad Nauseam
Keskowsow (Conversations in Cornish)
A Latin Legacy

PRINTED BY Book Printing UK

# Contents

# Acknowledgements

I should like to thank Dr Peter Jones of Friends of Classics and Dr Jenny March of the Classical Association for accepting articles for publication in their journals and so encouraging me (not a classicist by training) to compile the present book.

I must also thank Pan Macmillan and Mr. Colin Dexter for permission to include here extracts from Mr. Dexter's books.

In Memoriam
Selbie Campbell

# Food and Drink 1

*The Romans were noted for keeping a good table **ab ovo usque ad mala** (From the egg {mayonnaise} to the apples {Charlotte})*

### Ad nauseam
Suffering Juno, not peacock liver pâté again!

### Aegrotat
I don't think the asp tails in aspic agreed with Septimus

### Amari aliquid
I think this pomegranate juice has gone off

### Cave canem
I never eat boiled mastiff when there's an R in the month

### Detur digniori
Uncle Lucius's been working hard in the garden all day – he can have my spinach

### Disjecta membra
Uncle Claudius's making his usual hash of carving the bustard

### Festina lente
I know you're in a hurry, Minimus, but you chew those oysters well

### Nil volva pulchrius ampla
Nothing easier on the eye than a decent-sized sow's womb

### Sic volo, sic jubeo
I ordered the devilled dormice and the devilled dormice I want

### Vox et praeterea nihil
Hardly enough meat on a nightingale to warrant lighting the barbecue

# Food and Drink 2

*Since the Romans, the taste for food has not diminished*

### Ex nihilo nihil fit
Let's have some housekeeping money, then! Do you expect me to conjure up food out of thin air?

### Pudenda
First to eat all their spinach gets the parson's nose!

### Rara avis
Black swan? Ah! I thought it didn't taste like ordinary swan

### Ferae naturae
Someone left the lid off the snails' box, but I've cooked all I could catch

### Mutato nomine
We couldn't remember the name in Vietnamese so we rechristened it "Dong Hoi Muk"

### Facsimile
I can't believe this isn't real cucumber

### Flora
I can't believe this isn't Clover

### Tempus edax rerum
It's a new kind of tiramisu. Two days after its sell-by date, it self-destructs

### Tempus edax rerum
Don't worry, the leftovers will compost down

### Trivia
Trifles

### Veni, vidi, vici
I came to the carvery, and I admit my eyes were bigger than my stomach, but I managed to eat it all

# Food and Drink 3

*Cuisine since the Romans has, of course, become much more sophisticated*

### Nil volva pulchrius ampla
It's something Fortnum's have just begun stocking.  I'll tell you what it is after you've finished it

### Cum grano salis
I think a "tablespoonful of salt" in the recipe must have been a misprint

### E pluribus unum
It's spring vegetable soup

### Omnium gatherum
There's no recipe – I just put in anything I can lay my hands on

### Sui generis
It's a sort of one-off dish – I know I forgot one of the main ingredients but I can't remember which

### Mutatis mutandis
It's the same recipe but with red strawberry chillis instead of strawberries

### Feliciter audax
I got the recipe out of a 1935 copy of "Tit-bits" but I think it's turned out all right

### Mirabile dictu
You'll never believe this but they ate it all up

### De gustibus non est disputandum
I'm always so excited when people actually eat what I've cooked

### Cum omnibus suis pertinenciis
I'm so sorry, I must have forgotten to remove the giblets

### Fauna
I'm so sorry, I must have forgotten to wash the lettuce

### Caput mortuum
Darling, there's some funny sludge at the bottom of my glass

# Food and Drink 4

*But despite setbacks eating still remains popular*

**Benedictus benedicat**
Grace before meat

**Cornucopia**
A horn overflowing

**Multum in parvo**
A plate overflowing

**Panis angelicus**
Angel bread

**Placentae angelicae**
Angel cakes

**Elixir vitae**
This is what I call a pick-me-up!

**Pabulum**
I haven't tasted food like this since I was at school!

**De novo**
I could eat that all over again

**Consummatum est**
Sorry, that's the last of the spotted dick

**De profundis**
Sorry about the tummy rumbling

**Post hoc, ergo propter hoc**
He asked for the Mammoth Special and was up all night

**Gratias tibi agimus**
Grace after meat

# Party Time 1

*The old Roman orgiastic traditions have not wholly died out*

## Gaudeamus igitur, juvenes dum sumus
Let's live it up tonight because in the morning you're going to be feeling your age

## Panem et circenses
Tell you what, let's have nibbles *and* a stripper

## Persona non grata
Gate-crasher

## Integer vitae scelerisque purus
We'll get the vicar to be bouncer

## In loco parentis

Mum couldn't come to the party so I've brought Jacko instead

## Ave atque vale
Must you go?  You've only just come!

## Nescit vox missa reverti
Unfortunately we sent them the invitation the day before they ran over Spot.

## Party Time 2

*Repeat – the old Roman orgiastic traditions have not wholly died out*

### In toto
I made thirty-six shrimp vol-au-vents this morning and the wretched dog's eaten them all up

### Mea culpa
Oh dear, I think I've just trodden on your gerbil

### Requiescat in pace (R.I.P.)
Just leave it there. I'll scrape it up in the morning

### Habeas corpus
If you carry my husband out to the car, I'll drive him home

### A posteriori
Looking back, I suppose we should have had the break-dancing before supper

### Errare est humanum
No, the party was last night. We wondered why you didn't come

### Lapsus linguae
Did I say Saturday? Sorry, I should have said "Friday"

# In the Pub 1

*The Romans would have felt at home in a British pub*

## Nunc est bibendum
Cheers!

## Aqua pura
"All the water served in this establishment has been passed by the management"

## Cave uxorem
"Beware of the wife"

## Non compos mentis
"You don't have to be mad to work here but it helps"

## Dulce est desipere in loco
It's lovely to let your hair down in the local

## Aliquando bonus dormitat Homerus
Someone wake Homer up and tell him Marge wants another drink

## E pluribus unum
Now that's what I call a cocktail!

## Ex gratia
Dead newt? Not one of ours, squire. But have a fresh pint on the house

## Hic, haec, hoc
Percy's the only person I know can hiccup in three different registers

## In vinculis matrimonii
Sorry, pet, no can do – I've brought the wife along tonight

## Ne sit ancillæ tibi amor pudori
Cool, it, Frank, everyone falls in love with the barmaid

# In the Pub 2

*Repeat, the Romans would have felt very much at home in a British pub*

## Aegrotat
I don't think that last pint of Sangria agreed with Denzil

## In situ
I'm afraid I can't get up – my knees have gone all funny

## Ne plus ultra
No more for you, sweetie, seven vodkas is quite enough for one night

## Facilis descensus Averno
Absinthe? Ooh, I don't know. Well, all right, then, just a small one

## Perpetuum mobile
The bar's just going round and round

## Vade mecum
I don't think I'll make it to the loo unless you hold my hand

## Vis medicatrix naturae
I shall be all right once I get out in the fresh air

## Domus et placens uxor
If I don't get home soon, my wife will kill me

## Exeunt omnes
Closing time, please

## Holidays 1

*The Romans travelled most of the then known world*

**Dulce est desipere in loco**
It's party time on the Eurostar Express

**Parturiunt montes nascetur ridiculus mus**
We were halfway up Mount Etna and you'll never guess what happened!

**Mare nostrum**
I told him it was everybody's sea and we would pee in it if we wanted to

**In transitu**
Waring? He gave us all the slip somewhere in Bosnia. Isn't he home yet?

**O tempora, o mores**
Their clock time may be six hours ahead of ours but they have some *very* antiquated customs

**Solvitur ambulando**
The minibus broke down and we had to walk ten miles to the hotel

**Solvitur ambulando**
The ski-lift broke down and we had to walk 1500 feet to the ruddy top

**Per ardua ad astra**
The ski-lift broke down and we had to walk 1800 feet to the ruddy top

**Caelum non animum mutant qui trans mare currunt**
Souvenirs? You must be joking! Denis is just the same mean bastard on holiday as he is when he's at home.

**In absentia**
You'll never guess what happened while you were away

**Memento**
When I said "Bring me back some rock," I meant the kind you can eat

## Holidays 2

*Like the British the Romans were great sailors*

**Coitus plenus et optabilis**
I've never been away with such a friendly crowd before

**Afflavit Deus et dissipantur**
I hung out my knickers to dry on the ship's railing and they blew away

**Beneficium accipere libertatem est vendere**
All I did was take a piece of his Turkish Delight and I spent the next three weeks in his harem

**Ex Africa semper aliquid novi**
It's some unknown bug he picked up in Tripoli

**Media vita in morte sumus**
Well, he forgot to take his yellow fever pills, didn't he?

**Vox et praeterea nihil**
This is your Captain speaking

**Odi profanum vulgus et arceo**
Oh, we never mix with the other passengers

**Delenda est Carthago**
We quite liked Carthage, but I could gladly put a bomb under Benidorm

**Latet anguis in herba**
The second day out I found this ruddy great python in my lemon grass salad

**Splendide mendax**
I'll never believe a glossy brochure again

**Pabulum**
Next time I go on a luxury cruise, I'll pack sandwiches

**Praemonitus, praemunitus**
Thank God Gladys warned us to take our own toilet paper

**Holidays 3**

*But we get to places the Romans never dreamed of*

### Fons et origo
It was a thousand mile re-run on foot of Speke's discovery of the source of the Nile

### Impedimenta
We had a sort of basic holiday in Copacabana and our luggage had one of idle luxury in Casablanca

### Simplex munditiis
Edward said I looked divine in just a grass skirt

### Mons Veneris
At eleven thousand feet they claimed it was the highest bordello in South America

### Ultima Thule
It started off just fine as a routine cruise around Spitzbergen . . .

### Terra incognita
. . . the captain lost his way and we finished up God knows where

### Coitus interruptus
I thought the earth had moved but actually we'd hit an iceberg

### Multum in parvo
We had to pack twice as many people into the lifeboat as it was built for

### Vade mecum
You really must come with me next time

### Stella maris
Actually we're going to Broadstairs next year instead

**Holidays 4**

*And in other ways we've left the Romans far behind*

### Camera obscura
Snaps?  No.  We bought a video camera in Dubai but the
instructions were all in Arabic

### In camera
Snaps?  No.  Celia dropped the camera in her triggerfish chowder
and now all we get is "Access Denied"

### Timor mortis conturbat me
Geoffrey just lives for bungee-jumping from the Burj Khalifa, but
I've decided it isn't really my scene

### Bis peccare in saliendo elastico non licet
Geoffrey just lives for bungee-jumping from the Burj Khalifa, but
I've decided it isn't really my scene

### Locus standi
We had to stand in the guard's van all the way across Baluchistan

### Noctes ambrosianæ
I wouldn't say the food in Kyrgyzstan was monotonous exactly but
we did have tinned rice pudding for supper every night

### Mobile perpetuum
Twenty-three countries in seven days

### Mobile perpetuum
Our feet didn't touch the ground from Luton to Lusaka

### Taedium vitae
Once you've seen one monkey sanctuary you've seen the lot

### Excelsior
We're saving up for a holiday next year on a space station

# In the Gym 1

*The Romans placed a high value on physical fitness*

**Orandum est ut sit mens sana in corpore sano**
You must pray for a sound mind in a sound body, and it's clear that some of you are going to have to pray a lot harder than others

**Orare est laborare, laborare est orare**
Prayer is work, work is prayer, but I find prayer a lot less exhausting

**Acta non verba**
Please stop nattering and get on with your exercises

**Apparatus**
Apparatus

**Citius, Altius, Fortius**
Faster, higher, and give it a lot more wellie!

**Excelsior**
Higher!

**Est modus in rebus**
There is a middle course in everything and fifteen minutes is my limit

**Quam celerrime**
Speed it up, or we'll be here all ruddy night

**Perpetuum mobile**
Please, somebody, how the hell do you turn this treadmill off?

**Tityre, tu patulae recubans sub tegmine fagi**
I'm getting my old man to lift himself off his backside and come here and work off some fat

**Vis inertiae**
The power of inertia, of doing damn all, is my idea of exertion

## In the Gym 2

*The Romans must have been aware of the downside of PE*

### Pudenda

If you come off the beam, for Pete's sake make sure both your legs
are on the same side of it

### Disjecta membra
My arms feel as if they've dropped off

### Pede claudo
I'm limping because Gary dropped 150 kg on my foot

### Errare est humanum
I know I'm doing it all wrong but I'm only human

**Proxime accessit**
You nearly made it that time!  Try again

**Totis viribus**
I'm giving it all I've got!

**Ne plus ultra**
I know my limitations – do you want blood as well?

**Ultra vires**
Pull-ups?  Darling, it takes me all my strength to pull up my knickers

**Resurgam**
I shall get up off the floor again when I've had a little rest

**Fatigatus et aegrotus**
I'm tired and I'm feeling sick and I'm going home

**In articulo mortis**
Does anyone here do artificial respiration?

# Shopping

*It would seem that Rome had shops and so do we*

### Cacoethes emendi
The itch to go shopping,
endemic in half the population

### Caveat emptor
Our customers are *never* right

### Cornucopia
Our hypermarket sells everything under the sun

### Omnium gatherum
Our corner shop sells everything under the sun

### Arbiter elegantiarum
"How could she appear in public dressed like that?"

### De gustibus non est disputandum
"How could she appear in public dressed like that?"

### Coram populo
"How could she appear in public dressed like that?"

### Simplex munditiis
If she appeared in public in anything skimpier than that, she'd be
illegal

### Et in Arcadia ego
I got it in one of those marvellous shops in the Arcade

### Nunquam ubi sub ubi
No, I didn't forget to put any on – I just felt hot in 'em

### Sine qua non
Darling, you're simply not dressed without a Chanel handbag

### Multum in parvo
I think, Madam, perhaps you ought to try on something about four
sizes bigger

## Decus et tutamen

I know it looks like an ordinary strappy top but actually this one's
bullet-proof

### Modus vivendi
A way of living (together) in harmony,
having first agreed about who spends what

### Amantium irae amoris integratio est
By that reckoning they must be one of the most loving couples ever

### Casus belli
"That set you back how much, darling?"

### Denarius
Cheap at the price

## Nemo me impune lacessit

I'm carrying my weighted handbag
because I'm off to the sales

## Ne plus ultra
"I'm not setting foot in another bleeding shop"

## Fatigatus et aegrotus
"I'm not setting foot in another bleeding shop"

**Early Years**

**Gaudeamus igitur, juvenes dum sumus**
Let's pub it and club it while we're still young enough

**Ars longa, vita brevis**
"John Longbottom dies, aged 3 months"

**Ex Africa semper aliquid novi**
We're adopting two little girls from Chad

**Hinc illae lacrimae**
I told you to watch it with that nappy pin!

**Quid pro quo**

I'd gladly change this one for a hamster

**In loco parentis**
Can you recommend a good baby-sitter?

**In statu pupillari**
Teaching 11E is like talking to a bunch of statues

**Maxima debetur puero reverentia**
I suspect they've been hiring out Miles to the porn-brokers

**Matre pulchra filia pulchrior**
The mother's a stunner but the daughter's got the edge on her!

**Perpetuum mobile**
He took his first steps last week and now we can't get the little
bleeder to sit still

**Loquitur**
He said his first word yesterday, and now we can't get the little
bleeder to shut up

**Tabula rasa**
He said his first word yesterday, but we can't think where he picked
up that sort of language

**Ab incunabula**
I'm sorry Lauren set fire to your pashmina – that one's been
nothing but trouble from day one

**Virgo intacta**
We were offered a very good price for Natalie in Marrakech, but we
decided her GCSE's came first

**Vox et praeterea nihil**
Only a pound and a half at birth but what a pair of lungs!

**Virginibus puerisque**
What with the shaved heads, tattoos and nose rings, I reckon they
must be the only unisex family in Horsham

## On The Road

*The Romans would have been hard put to recognise their roads nowadays*

### Favete linguis
Belt up

### In vinculis
I couldn't unfasten my safety belt

### Citius, Altius, Fortius
The revamped Olympia Pegasus features a seven-litre engine, retractable wings and carbon-steel bull-bars

### Rigor mortis
The engine just seized up

### Media vita in morte sumus
We were stuck for three hours in the outside lane of the M25

### Post mortem
The garage are taking the engine to bits now

### Consummatum est
I wonder if they still do a scrappage scheme?

### Coitus plenus et optabilis
We always use a nice little out-of-the-way lay-by

### Coitus interruptus
We'd switched our lights off, and this lorry driver didn't see us when he drove into the lay-by

### Post coitum triste
The Fire Brigade had to cut us out of the back seat. So embarrassing

**Fiat**
No. It's a Lamborghini

**Fiat lux**
I think you'll find it easier to see where you're going if you switch
on your headlights

**Siste viator**
Honey, you're supposed to stop for people on zebra crossings

**Alea iacta est**
No, you can't practise your three-point turn here – it's a one-way
street

**Video meliora proboque; deteriora sequor**
I should have stuck to the main road but the satnav knew a short cut

**Status quo ante**
Ah, we seem somehow to have got back to where we started

**Via Dolorosa**
Sorry we're late – we were stuck for seventeen miles behind a
hearse

**Amari aliquid**
We stopped for coffee at the Fonte Leporum Services

**In medias res**
We weren't part of the original accident but we didn't see it in time
and we hit a fire engine

**Stet**
No need to move the car yet – there's another ten minutes on the
meter

**Tempus fugit**
Look, mate, the clock on this meter must be running fast

**Omnibus**
Bus

**Omnium gatherum**
Car Park Full

**Omnium gatherum**
We hit gridlock at Hyde Park Corner

**Supera moras**
Fifty quid extra for you if you make Gatwick by eight twenty

**Quam celerrime**
Sixty quid on top if you make Heathrow by eight forty

**Per se**
This car practically drives itself

**Impedimenta**
Eventually we found Emily in the boot – she'd got mixed up with
the suitcases

**Facilis descensus Averno**
We were halfway down the hill to the ferry when the brakes failed

**Festina lente**
Where's the fire at, sir?

**Quo vadis**
And where do you think you might be going, sir?

**Tandem**
Who's driving this ruddy bike, you or me?

**Timor mortis conturbat me**
I don't let Hilary drive now

**In situ**
We haven't been out in the car since somebody pinched the wheels

### In Vinculis Matrimonii *At Home*

### Desiderata
I've managed to get the wedding list down to twelve web pages

### Pervigilium Veneris
The scars?  Let's just say it was quite a stag night

### Ad libitum
The only advice Mummy gave me for my wedding night was
"Play it by ear"

### Ius primae noctis

The squire's gone home, darling, but now I've got this splitting
headache

### Amantium irae amoris integratio est
Darling I'll always love you, and I promise not to throw the cat
litter tray at you again

### Bis peccare in bello non licet
I'll forgive you this once, my precious, but you do it again, you're
in deep doo-doo

### Si vis pacem, para bellum
Look, darling, Auntie Mabel's sent us a loaded rolling-pin

### Dies irae, dies illa
Friday's not usually a very good day for Chris – I find it pays to tread rather carefully

### Persona non grata
I've made up a bed for your mother in the shed

### Fragrat post funera virtus
How long have these prawns been under the fridge?

### Lustrum
Darling, don't you think it's time you had a bath?

### Suum cuique bene olet
Darling, I wish you'd spray the airwick when you've been in the bathroom

### Sunt lacrimae rerum
No, I'm perfectly happy – I've just been peeling onions

### Non est inventus
How can you lose a hot-water-bottle in a one-bedroomed flat?

### In vacuo
Of course the cat's looking cross.  So would *you* be looking cross if I'd caught *your* tail in the hoover

### Lusus naturae
Have you seen our new neighbour?

### Lares et penates
The china slugs?  I know they're ugly but they're heirlooms – Aunt Hester said they always brought her luck

### Lapsus linguae
Are you going deaf or something?  I said "PRISCILLA"!

### Non compos mentis
It's Auntie Maia on the phone, darling.  Do you want to talk to her?

### Tertium quid
Darling, I'm sure there's somebody under the bed

### De Profundis
Grandpa's got a pad down in the cellar but we have him up for
Sunday lunch

### Modus vivendi
Suppose you do it your way and let me do it mine

### Modus operandi
Suppose you do it your way and let me do it mine

### Non sequitur
I don't follow you, darling. Could you go over it all again from the
beginning?

### De novo
I don't follow you, darling. Could you go over it all again from the
start?

### Ab initio
Mummy told me the secret of a successful marriage was to put your
foot down from day one

### Quota
Go to sleep, darling. You've had your ration of cous-cous for this
week

## Senecta Molesta– *A troubled old age*

### Dulce domum
Welcome to The Briars Care Home for the Elderly

### Ferae naturae
I'm not sure we're going to get on with the new matron

### O dea certe
I've a feeling we're going to get on all right with the new nurse

### Pabulum
When I say the meals here are out of this world, I mean they're like nothing on earth

### Non est inventus
Could you look and see if I've dropped my teeth under the bed?

### Ex voto
When I left my mother's knee I swore I would never touch mutton again, and that vow still stands

### Quid pro quo
I'll swap you two sprouts for a carrot

### Addenda
Could you be an angel and put some HP sauce on my cabbage?

### Ab ovo
I've just come across an earwig in my boiled egg

### Tabula rasa
Since I drank that coffee my mind's gone a complete blank

### Dum spiro spero
If I wake up and find I've stopped breathing overnight, that's when I start to worry

### Non omnis moriar
I've bequeathed my kidneys to Barnado's

### In situ
Mildred's been sitting there for three days now.  Do you think there's anything wrong?

### Requiescat in pace
For God's sake don't wake her up – she'll only start talking again

### Habeas corpus

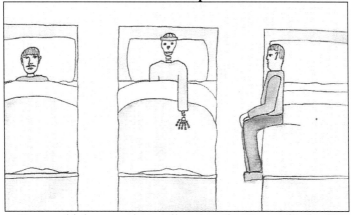

Do you think we ought to tell matron that Bernard's dead?

### Persona non grata
Here comes Verbal Diarrhoea again

### Pede claudo
Allow me to introduce Pegleg Pete

### Alias
We shan't be able to remember Indra – whatever you said – we'll have to call you Jane

### Sine nomine
He told us he'd forgotten his name – we call him Number Nine

### Compos mentis
I wasn't born yesterday

### O mihi praeteritos
Surrounded by all these beautiful nurses and I haven't the strength
even to wolf-whistle

### Vixi puellis nuper idoneus
Surrounded by all these beautiful nurses and I haven't the strength
even to wolf-whistle

### In flagrante delicto
Old Willoughby and the new nurse?  Bully for him!

### Coitus interruptus
Rumour hath it he fell asleep in the middle of it

### Tandem

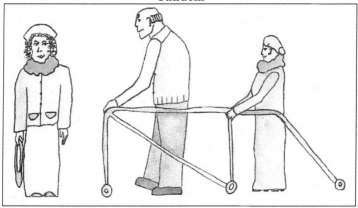

I had it custom-built so as I can nip any of his hanky-panky in the
bud

## Pari passu

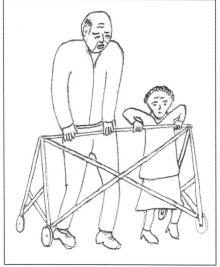

If you don't start taking longer steps, we'll be going round in circles
for ever

### In vinculis
We have to keep him handcuffed to his Zimmer now – he's lost
three since Christmas

### Vade mecum
Put your arms round my waist – my Zimmer's up to taking two

### Festina lente
No hurry.  This Zimmer wasn't built for speed

### Quam celerrime
My Zimmer's got three speeds – slow, dead slow and stop

### Perpetuum mobile
I hear they're going to install a treadmill for Zimmer training

### Fons et origo
The trouble all started when they brought in that time and motion
study fellow

# Per ardua ad astra

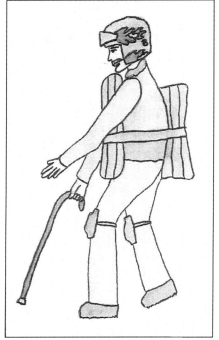

They've asked me to test-drive the new stair-lift

## Simplex munditiis
It's my shroud.  I thought I might as well get used to wearing it

## Felix qui potuit
I think I've found out what's been eating my toe nails

## Noli me tangere
I shouldn't touch me – my skin seems to be going green

## Rigor vitae
After last Thursday's line-dancing I just seized up completely

## Tempus fugit
It can't be Saturday today – we haven't had Friday yet

### Tempus edax rerum
So far I've lost all my hair, all my teeth, an eye, two fingers, half a
liver, and a leg.  I just wonder what's going to go next

### Pudenda
I can't find it in the latest edition of the Scrabble dictionary – can
you change it to "aunt"?

### Ad nauseam
It's the fifth year running the Prison Visitor's read us the whole of
"War and Peace"

### Abiit, excessit, evasit, erupit
They can't find Rupert.  They think he might have broken out
during the night

### Ultima Thule
There's a rumour they're going to close this place down and move
us all up to Wick

# VOX ROMANA 2

I hope the following pages throw some light on the Latin headings on the foregoing pages.

**Abiit, excessit, evasit, erupit**  *He has gone, he is fled, he has eluded our watch, he has broken through our guards*

The resourceful escaper was Catiline who had plotted to overthrow the government of Rome.  However, being accused of treason, he had deemed it prudent to get out of Rome quick and join his army of rebels in Etruria.  [N.B.  There appears to be no word in Latin, or in any other known language, for "escapee".]  Cicero clearly wanted to leave his hearers in little doubt that Catiline had in fact gone away, and in doing so offered to posterity a choice of four ways in which to say "he's scarpered" in Latin.

> "He [*sc.* the pig] bolts!  He's off! – *Evasit! Erupit!*"
> Leigh Hunt, "On the Graces and Anxieties of Pig-driving".

## Ab incunabulo  *From the cradle*

*Ab incunabulo* is much the same as *ab initio* and *ab ovo*, *qq.v.* "Incunabula" were originally "swaddling clothes", with the meaning later transferred to one's birth-place or one's origins. Later still the term "incunabula" was used to designate the earliest books printed in the West, (before 1st January 1501), that is, in the very infancy of printing from fixed type.

Sadly the "swaddling clothes" mentioned in the Gospel story of the birth of Jesus are rendered in the Vulgate simply and unromantically not as *incunabula* but as *panni* or "cloths".  The infant Jesus was swaddled *in pannis*.

## Ab initio  *From the beginning, at the outset*

Kipling in "The Propagation of Knowledge" placed his finger on the earliest roots of the Irish Problem.  "I tell you, Gillett, if the Romans had dealt faithfully with the Celt, *ab initio*, this – this would never have happened."

A tale recited *ab initio* gladdens the hearts of such as the King of Hearts in *Alice in Wonderland*, who tells the White Rabbit to: "Begin at the beginning and go on until you come to the end: then stop."

*Ab initio* refers to the initial stages of flying training and is the motto of No. 1 Elementary Flying School of the R.A.F.

In science *ab initio* means "from first principles". The Internet throws light on such recondite things as "*ab initio* programs for molecular electronic structure calculations"; and the firm "*Ab initio* software" have produced a unique administration package specifically for the Double-Glazing Industry.

## Ab origine *From the beginning, from the source*

Aboriginal inhabitants of a country, or *aborigines* ("abos" to some), have evolved there over millenia, or at least have been minding their own business there for a long time, in contrast to later immigrants.

The St. John's first annual Children's Art Show on Environmental Concerns, for young artists between the ages of 5 and 17 years of age, had the theme *Ab Origine.*

"These ladies sat side by side with young females destined to be *demoiselles de magazins*, and with some Flamandes, genuine aborigines of the country." Charlotte Brontë, *The Professor.*

In a book review in *The Guardian*, Mary Hoffman notes that from about the eighth century B.C. the Venetians traded salt from the marshes: "Venetians were merchants *ab origine.*"

## Ab ovo usque ad mala *From the egg (or from the start) to the apples (the finish)*

*Ab Ovo* is not only a French electronic duet, and a Latvian rhythm, beat and ethnic project headed by Nils Ile, but also an IT and engineering consulting firm based in Santa Clara, Ca, which claims to be a fast-growing, innovative and independent ICT services and products provider.

On its own *ab ovo* suggests a bird popping out of the egg, and may be used synonymously with such phrases as *ab initio, ab incunabulo* and *ab origine*, but Horace used *ab ovo usque ad mala* to define a feast which begins with an egg and finishes off with apples. *Ab ovo usque ad mala* can also be a wry comment on your friend and mine who monopolises the conversation at a meal from start to finish.

"Do you suppose that [dinner-time] is a pleasant period, and that we are to criticize you between the *ovum* and the *malum*, between the soup and the dessert?" W. M. Thackeray, *Roundabout Papers*. (Note that *mala* is the plural of *malum*, "an apple".)

### Acta non verba *Deeds not words*

This can loosely be translated as "War, war, not jaw, jaw", and is a motto which, being short and easy to spell, must have appealed to families who preferred the relaxed life of the hunting field to the more strenuous pursuits of reading and writing. It is the motto of several families, among them the Jameson family. Sir Leander Starr Jameson put the motto into practice and the family name into history in December 1895 by leading the "Jameson Raid" into the Transvaal in the hope of stirring up rebellion against the president, "Oom" Paul Kruger. He failed, but his attempt apparently inspired Rudyard Kipling to write his poem "If –".

### Addenda *Things which are to be added*

The endings "-anda" and "-enda" denote the "gerundive" of the verb, indicating that something has to be done, as in agenda, corrigenda, propaganda, pudenda, videnda, etc. "Addenda" is plural: if a single item only has to be added, this is an "addendum".

### Ad infinitum *To infinity*

There are no set bounds to *ad infinitum*. Sir Timothy Shelley, the father of Percy Bysshe (the budding poet), seems to have had little doubt about the limitless potential of his son for getting girls into trouble. It is said that he told young Percy he would provide for any "natural" children *ad infinitum*, but that he would never consent to his son's marrying beneath him. I am not sure whether Sir Timothy was ever called on to make good his promise and pay up, (or indeed whether young Percy fulfilled his potential in this field), but when the latter was nineteen, he eloped with sixteen-year-old Harriet Westbrook, without the paternal blessing.

The invention of the microscope allowed biologists to study life on earth at much closer quarters than before. Several reported that "Great fleas have little fleas upon their backs to bite 'em, And little fleas have lesser fleas, and so *ad infinitum*."

**Ad libitum (ad lib)** *At pleasure*

If you are offered something *ad libitum*, you are free to accept or to reject it as the fancy takes you. Written on a doctor's prescription, the abbreviation *ad lib* means "to be taken freely".

In a stage play, an *ad lib* is a line or comment which does not appear in the script, but which the actor speaks notwithstanding, at his own pleasure if not at that of the director. Cynics claim that most lines spoken by most actors are in fact ad libs.

John Ayto, writing in *The Observer*, noted that television newsreaders used the phrase "explanation into" in three successive bulletins, "so it was presumably a faithful representation of the written autocue, not an *ad-lib* aberration".

**Ad nauseam** *Until it makes you sick*

Variety is the spice of life and hearing the same old spiel repeated over and over again can prompt in the listener not only nausea but also murderous propensities. "In his dotage, Uncle Walter was given to recounting *ad nauseam* his wartime exploits in the Navy. In the end we half wished he had been vouchsafed a heroic and watery grave along with the less fortunate of his shipmates." P. J. Dorricot, *Nursery Tales*.

A book review in *The Guardian* noted that Marco Pierre White rarely mentioned taste and flavour in his discussion of cooking. "What he does bang on about, *ad nauseam*, is the look of a plate."

(Arthur Askey had a girl-friend called Nausea Bagwash. Had the couple flourished in ancient Rome, his collected love letters to her might have been published under the title "*Ad Nauseam*" – "To Nausea", but that is not quite the same thing.)

**Aegrotat** *He is ill*

Anyone too jittery or too drunk (or even too ill) to sit the final examination for a university degree, but whose work up to that point has shown enough merit, may on that evidence alone be granted the degree. His or her name will appear on the pass list, accompanied by the word *ægrotat*.

On the title page of Sellar and Yeatman's *1066 and All That,* Walter Carruthers Yeatman's accreditation appears as "Aegrot: Oxon:"

[Passed by virtue of illness at Oxford]. (*Vide "fatigatus et ægrotus" infra.*)

**Afflavit Deus et dissipantur** *God breathed and they are scattered*

After the Spanish Armada had been blown away from the south coast of Britain in 1588, to the mixed chagrin and relief of Francis Drake and his men, a medal bearing the words *Afflavit Deus et dissipantur,* "God breathed and they are dispersed" (note: "dispersed", not "dissipated"), was struck in celebration and handed out to Drake and Co. to compensate them for their disappointment.

This wasn't the last or only time the foreigner fell foul of Britain's weather. The words *Afflavit Deus et dissipantur* appeared also on a medal struck in 1797 to commemorate the dispersal by storms of a French invasion fleet off Bantry Bay in County Cork.

**Alea iacta est** *The die is cast*

At this point there is no turning back. Julius Caesar is said by Plautus to have quoted this proverbial saying (in its original Greek form, ανερριφθω κυβος, "*anerrhiphtho kubos*", derived from Menander) after crossing the Rubicon with his legions on 10th January, 49 B.C. (A.U.C. 705). He should have told his soldiers at this point to fall out and go home, and then have gone on to Rome *solus*, but considering what happened to him eventually, he could hardly be blamed for neglecting to disband his bodyguard. But by so crossing the Rubicon, the "point of no return", he rejected the authority of the Senate and precipitated the civil war between himself and Pompey.

For some reason *Alea Iacta Est* is the name of a research training programme network in tissue engineering.

**Alias (dictus)** *At another time (under a different name)*

We seem to be in danger of losing the useful word *alias* to the unattractive Americanism "aka" – "also known as". In the choice of which term to use, time is of the essence. Yusuf Islam was formerly known as "Cat Stevens" but if he no longer chooses to use this name, then he is "Yusuf Islam, *alias* Cat Stevens". If on the other hand he is Yusuf Islam in private but is still Cat Stevens when performing, then, fair enough, he is "aka Cat Stevens". Fortunately "aka" has as yet no plural, so we are forced instead to use *alias* in such statements as "Jones travelled under a variety of aliases" even though *alias* has no plural in Latin.

### Aliquando bonus dormitat Homerus  *Even good Homer nods at times*

Homer nodded off permanently a good while back but this phrase still rings bells today: for "Homer" substitute the name of any cricket umpire. Although the comment is often used to excuse someone's unforced errors, it is in fact a variant on a critical remark of Horace: *Indignor quandoque bonus dormitat Homerus* – "I deem it unworthy of him if Homer, usually good, nods for a moment." Horace will happily accept human frailty in any artist: but Homer? – no excuses; from him only the best will do.

". . . for if *aliquando bonus dormitat Homerus*, they should remember how long he stayed awake . . ." Miguel Cervantes, *Don Quixote*.

### Amantium irae amoris integratio est  *Lovers' quarrels are the renewal of love*

This is perhaps one of the most pathetically optimistic statements to have come down to us from the Latin writers, and probably more loving couples have fallen out arguing about it than for any other reason. Nevertheless a Latin T-shirt website offers a shirt with the inscription *Amantium irae amoris integratio est* as "a gift for your lover after an argument".

W. M. Thackeray heads chapter 66 of *Vanity Fair* and Anthony Trollope heads chapter 73 of *Phineas Finn* with *Amantium Iræ.*

In *The Oxford Book of English Verse* Richard Edwardes' poem "In going to my naked bed" is given the heading *Amantium Irae.* The last line of each stanza reads: "The falling out of faithful friends renewing is of love."

### Amari aliquid  *Something bitter*

This is a snippet from a longer piece by Lucretius, which runs: *Medio de fonte leporum surgit amari aliquid quod in ipsis floribus angat* – "From the depths of this fountain of delights wells up some bitter taste which chokes them even amid the flowers".

" 'A pity that Bingley is flourishing like a green what-is-it, but one can't have everything.'

'No, sir. *Medio de fonte leporum surgit amari aliquid in ipsis floribus angat.*' " P. G. Wodehouse, *Much Obliged, Jeeves.*

Coleridge uses the first seven of these words as the preface to his cautionary poem of "Julia", in which an ardent lover flings himself upon his knees before Julia and in so doing squashes her lap-dog.

"Yes, indeed, it was a delightful little holiday; it lasted a whole week. With the exception of that little pint of *aliquid amari* at Rotterdam, we were all very happy." W. M. Thackeray, *Roundabout Papers.*

*Amari Aliquid* is the name of the Viskr Aspect of the Kumoti (Wyld) Faction of the Ananasi werespiders.

**Apologia** *A vindication*

In 1864 Cardinal John Newman wrote an account of his life and opinions under the title *Apologia pro Vita Sua* – "A defence of the conduct of his life". Over the years the term "apology" has acquired connotations of guilt, of *mea culpa*, but the original *apologia* was in no sense apologetic.

**A posteriori** *From events coming after*

*A Posteriori* is the title of a studio album of New Age electronic music by a German Group "Enigma".

*A posteriori* reasoning identifies causes "by studying the clear results of sensory experience", which smacks a little of *post hoc, propter hoc (q.v.)* reasoning, but which it seems is very respectable in the realm of philosophy.

"That it was Yorick's and no one's else: – It was proved to be so, *a posteriori*, the day after, when Yorick sent a servant to my Uncle Toby's house, to enquire after it." Laurence Sterne, *Tristram Shandy.*

**Apparatus** *Things prepared*

English writers lifted the word "apparatus" directly from Latin, but, being a fourth declension noun, *apparatus* as written may be either singular or plural. (This was no problem to the Romans since they pronounced the word differently in the singular and in the plural, with a short "u" and long "u" respectively.) We rarely talk about "an apparatus", though there is no reason why we should not do so. Both "The apparatus is broken" and "The apparatus are broken" are equally correct. The usual way of avoiding the dilemma is to talk about a "piece of apparatus".

At a point in my National Service training, we were shown how to fall flat on our faces ready to fire our rifles. Our ever-considerate corporal Mike told us to "grasp the rifle firmly in the left hand and fall forward on to the right hand, being careful to avoid the wedding apparatus as you go down."

### Aqua pura *Pure water*

This is water from the spring, uncontaminated and fit to drink, and hence is also known (though not perhaps widely) as *aqua fontana*. In many ways it is similar to water obtained from the tap or from the bottle. The schoolboy howler analyses it: "Water is made up of two gins, oxygin and hydrogin. Oxygin is pure gin, but hydrogin is gin and water."

*Aqua Pura* is the title of a CD produced by the group "Dyed Emotions".

*Nil Sine Aqua* – "Nothing Without Water" – was the stating-the-obvious motto of the South Staffordshire Waterworks Company.

### Arbiter elegantiarum *A judge of matters of taste*

Every age requires its trend-setter. Tacitus designated Petronius as *elegantiæ arbiter,* of which *arbiter elegantiarum* is a later variant.

"In his inmost heart he desired to be something more than a mere *arbiter elegantiarum*, to be consulted on the wearing of a jewel, or the knotting of a necktie, or the conduct of a cane." Oscar Wilde, *The Picture of Dorian Gray.*

"In the 1950's, Mrs. Lillicrap, who made her own clothes copied from pictures in the fashion magazines, was our neighbourhood *arbiter elegantiarum.*" P. J. Dorricot, *Beyond the Nursery Slopes.*

Henry Fielding in *Tom Jones* introduces an arbiter of another kind, "Heydegger, the great *arbiter deliciarum*, the great high priest of pleasure."

**Ars longa, vita brevis** *Art is long, life is short,* or *So long a time to learn the art, so short a time to live*

This is Hippocrates in despairing mood, quoted by Seneca. The art, as one might suppose of Hippocrates, was the art of healing. The phrase does *not* mean "a short skirt on a fat bottom". On the other hand *Punch* magazine once commented on an obituary notice: "John Longbottom, aged 3 months, dies: *Ars longa vita brevis.*"

Sir John Millais took *Ars longa, vita brevis* as his family motto. Longfellow translated it as: "Art is long but time is fleeting". *Vita Brevis* is the title of a book by Jostein Gaarder, and *Ars Longa Vita Brevis* is the name of the 2nd album by the English progressive rock group The Nice.

**Ave atque vale** *Hail and farewell*

Catullus visited his brother's tomb near Troy for the first time while on his way to Bithynia. Not planning to pass that way again, he said: *Atque in perpetuum, frater, ave atque vale* – "And so for ever, brother, hail and farewell". (*Ave atque vale* was in fact a traditional Roman farewell to the dead.)

*Ave atque Vale* is the official website of the book on the history of the Vale-Special sports car.

Colin Dexter heads the final chapter of *The Jewel that was Ours* with the poem's last two lines: *Accipe fraterno multum manantia fletu Atque in perpetuum, frater, ave atque vale.* "Accept [these gifts] drenched with many a brotherly tear, And so, etc."

Tennyson, sympathizing with Catullus, wrote a poem entitled "Frater Ave atque Vale". Had the film "Brief Encounter" been made in ancient Rome, its title might well have been "Ave atque Vale".

**Benedictus benedicat** *May the Blessed One give a blessing*

A brief form of Latin grace used in colleges and places where they use Latin and eat.

" '*Benedictus benedicat, per Jesum Christum Dominum nostrum,*' [Mr. Thursley] said at last in his praying voice, which was deep . . . and charged with transcendental significance." Aldous Huxley, *Eyeless in Gaza.*

**Beneficium accipere libertatem est vendere**  *To accept a favour is to sell one's liberty*

Around 50 B.C. Publilius Syrus published a number of profound and witty thoughts under the title of *Sententiae*, of which this was one. It clearly struck a chord in a sufficient number of rueful and captive minds to be bandied about as a warning from then onwards. However, judging by estimates of the high incidence of official and commercial corruption world-wide, the value placed on liberty seems sometimes not to amount to very much.

*Sententiae* were thoughts cast into the form of maxims or aphorisms, and were the sort of thing one might find in a Roman Christmas cracker, had such crackers existed. The word "maxim" itself derives from the phrase *maxima sententia*, a "greatest thought", or as one might say, a "lofty thought". In 1920 H. L. Menken published a collection of his own witticisms in a book which he called *Sententiae*.

**Bis peccare in bello non licet**  *In war one may not blunder twice*

"He pressed upon me the importance of planting [trees] at the first in a very sufficient manner, quoting the saying, *In bello non licet bis errare*; and adding, 'this is equally true in planting.' "  James Boswell. *The Life of Samuel Johnson, LL.D.* (*Peccare* is "to sin", *errare* is "to err".)

A variant of this warning is *Bis peccare in saliendo elastico non licet*, or "In bungee-jumping one may not blunder twice."

In the theatre or the concert hall, "Bis!" – "twice", is of course the French for "Encore!"

**Cacoethes scribendi**  *An itch for writing*

"*Cacoethes*" is not Latin but Greek, and was adopted into Latin by the normal process of language borrowing. The phrase is used by Juvenal, who is scathing about it – *insanabile cacoethes scribendi* – "the incurable itch for writing."  The Irish poet Samuel Lover (1797–1868) expands on this and offers some hope of relief: "When once the itch of literature comes over a man, nothing can cure it but the scratching of a pen. (But if you have not a pen, I suppose you must scratch any way you can.)"  There is a writers' group called "Cacoethes-Scribendi".

Other cognate phrases are *cacoethes loquendi*, an itch for talking, and *cacoethes emendi*, an itch for going shopping, both being endemic in half the population, one might almost say from scratch.

**Caelum non animum mutant qui trans mare currunt**   *They change their skies but not their souls who flee across the sea*

This is Horace speaking. *Caelum* is sometimes spelled as *coelum*, which is said to be an error perpetrated in the Middle Ages and perpetuated ever since, so that the standard dictionaries of Latin use *coelum* in preference to *caelum*. The preference extended to the Latin used in the Roman Catholic church, as in *Regina Coeli*, "Queen of Heaven".

*Caelum non Animum* is the motto of several families, including Harper of Lamberts and Rhodes of Bellair.

Milton had a similar thought to Horace's; but whereas Horace's smacks much of the despair of one who by travelling is trying unsuccessfully to escape from the trammels of his own thoughts, Milton's gives boundless hope of mental freedom:

"The mind is its own place and in itself
Can make a Heav'n of Hell, a Hell of Heav'n." – *Paradise Lost*,
Book I.

**Camera obscura**   *A darkened room*

This is not the "dark room" in which camera film is (was?) developed, but a darkish space, sometimes no more than a mere box, in which an image from the outside world is projected on to a screen *via* a series of lenses.

*Camera Obscura* is the name of a Scottish indie pop band from Glasgow.

"The landscape has not the hues of the real world; it is modified in the *camera obscura* of the self-enclosed intelligence." W. Bagehot, *Literary Studies*, "Percy Bysshe Shelley".

**Caput mortuum** *A dead head*

But not so much a dead head as a dead bottom. *Caput mortuum* is "the inert residuum left by a process of chemical distillation or sublimation", or, to put it more succinctly, "sludge".

> "This is the caput mortuum of pain:
> Perhaps your splinters have a power to prickle . . .
> They are not pain, for pain is spiritual. . . ."
>
> Alan Porter, "The Signature of Pain".

*Brewer's Dictionary of Phrase and Fable* suggests that "the French Directory, towards its close, was a mere *caput mortuum* of a governing body."

*Caput mortuum* is the name given to the pigment Cardinal Purple, derived from iron rust. It was also the name given to "Mummy Brown", a pigment made from ground-up mummified bodies, once used widely by artists until they found out where it came from.

**Carpe diem** *Reap the harvest of the day*

It is difficult to walk the streets of any large town nowadays and not come across these words emblazoned on a T-shirt, the wearer presumably hoping to come across a kindred spirit anxious to make the most of what was to be reaped before the day was out. The complete thought is *Carpe diem quam minimum credula postero* – "Reap the harvest of the day, trust as little as possible in the morrow".

Many poets have written poems in the spirit of "Gather ye rosebuds while ye may" and "Youth's a stuff will not endure." Lawrence Hope gave the title *Carpe Diem* to one of his poems, while Byron uses the phrase in the last stanza of "Don Juan":

> "But *carpe diem*, Juan, *carpe, carpe*!
> Tomorrow sees another race as gay
> And transient, and devour'd by the same harpy . . ."

Erskine Childers in *The Riddle of the Sands* adapts the phrase, casting it in the subjunctive mood for "let us make the most of the day": "We abandoned ourselves, three youthful, hungry mariners, to the enjoyment of this impromptu picnic. Such a chance might never occur again – *carpamus diem*."

Evidence that *Carpe Diem* has caught the public imagination so as to become almost a mantra lies in the fact that at least two commercial firms have adopted the title. One "Carpe Diem" offers "Celebration Parchments" for weddings and similar landmark events in one's lifetime: another offers "botanic water", presumably for serving up instead of champagne at weddings and similar landmark events in one's lifetime. The cogent argument that champagne itself has botanic origins seems churlish in the face of the enthusiasm the producers have for their own product, foreshadowed by Hippocrates two and a half thousand years ago in a treatise on the incomparable benefits of herbal brews.

**Casus belli**  *A reason for war, for dispute*

The invasion of Belgium in 1914 and of Poland in 1939, and the threat of weapons of mass destruction in Iraq at a later date, are all examples of a *casus belli*.

The term is also used in non-combatant circles. Adrian Hamilton, writing in *The Observer*, said: "Yesterday the *casus belli* was the Social Charter, today it is the budget."

*Casus* is a fourth declension noun like *apparatus* (*q.v.*), and the plural of *casus belli* is also *casus belli*. John Fowles in *A Maggot* reports that an inquiry dealt with heriot and farleu, thraves and cripplegaps, plowbote and wainbote, hedge-scouring and whin-drawing "(and a hundred other obscure *casus belli* between landlord and tenant); . . ."

**Caveat Emptor**  *Let the buyer beware*

No one can possibly have not met with this maxim in Latin law, of universal relevance, and even more pertinent today. The writer of a letter to *The Guardian* pointed out that "eBay itself is plastered with 'caveat emptor' warnings."

*Caveat Emptor* is the name of a book written by Ken Perenyi, a master American art forger.

But as well as the buyer, the reader may also be vulnerable. Sara Wheeler, reviewing a book on Iran for *The Guardian,* noted that before an essay on the origins and history of Islamic art, "[the author] inserts a caveat lector advising uninterested readers to skip to the next chapter."

**Cave canem**  *Beware of the dog*

This brief warning was found written in mosaic on the portal of a house excavated in the ruins of Pompeii. It is quoted by Petronius but dates back to the Greeks if not to the first cave-dwellers.

James Thurber in "The Dog That Bit People" recorded that they buried the dog along a lonely road, putting up a smooth board above his grave on which they wrote with an indelible pencil 'Cave Canem'. "Mother was quite pleased with the simple classic dignity of the old Latin epitaph."

Reports of sightings of the variants *Cave felem* – "Beware of the cat", and *Cave uxorem* – "Beware of the wife", are apocryphal.

**Citius, Altius, Fortius**  *Faster, higher, stronger*

This is the motto of the Olympic Games, presented in Latin presumably because it is a safe neutral language, even if few people can understand it. (A book on setting up a website suggests that using Latin text in a mock-up page helps you concentrate on the design: you can download Latin/pseudo-Latin text from www.lipsum.com. Again, Latin is a nice neutral language.)

**Coitus interruptus**  *Interrupted intercourse*

*Coitus interruptus* is a method of birth control by withdrawing the *membrum virile* before ejaculation. Its effectiveness compares well with that of the rhythm method.

*Coitus interruptus* usually starts as great sex (*vide "Coitus plenus et optimabilis" infra*) but may then be cut short either voluntarily or involuntarily for any one of a thousand reasons, the three most common being :

   a)   an interested and aggrieved third party bursting in on the busy couple;

   b)   a fire alarm and especially the activation of the sprinkler system;

   c) cramp.

Colin Dexter, in *The Remorseful Day*, states that before she was murdered the dead woman had a client in bed with her, "and if ever there was a *locus classicus* for what they call *coitus interruptus* this was it, because someone interrupted the proceedings."

**Coitus plenus et optabilis** *Perfect and desirable coitus*

*Coitus plenus et optabilis* is great sex – plenty of it and just what was hoped for, the sort of thing we would have asked Santa for as kids had we had an inkling of what sensual pleasures lay ahead of us once licking lollipops had lost its allure.

"She had taken deep pleasure in sex until it became a hobby with almost slogan proportions: *coitum plenum et optabilem.*" Richard Condon, *Arigato.* (It isn't clear why Condon puts the phrase in the accusative case rather than in the nominative, unless it's in remote apposition to "pleasure".)

**Compos mentis** *Of sound mind*

*Vide "Non compos mentis" infra*

**Consummatum est** *It is finished*

The last words of Christ on the cross (John xix. 30). It is likely that Christ spoke the words in Aramaic, his native tongue, but it seems difficult to find out exactly what they would have been in this language. In the Greek of St. John's Gospel they are the single word τετελεσται, *"tetelestai"*. Marlowe puts the words *Consummatum est* into the mouth of Dr. Faustus as he finishes writing the bill of sale of his soul to Lucifer.

*Consummatum Est* is the name of a band formed in Italy at the end of 2003. The music they played was black metal with gothic influences but in 2004 they changed their music style and become a doom metal band. *Consummatum est* is also the title of a sculpture by Jacob Epstein in the National Gallery of Scotland.

**Coram populo** *Before people, in public*

Horace used this phrase in his *Ars Poetica* (line 185) when he suggested that certain dramatic business should be conducted off-stage rather than enacted on-stage. The two relevant lines run:

*Ne pueros coram populo Medea trucidet,*
*Aut humana palam coquat exta nefarius Atreus.*
Let not Medea slaughter her boys in full view of the audience,
Nor wicked Atreus openly cook human entrails.

(Atreus had killed his brother's sons and served them up to his unsuspecting brother as a tasty dish.)

Horace did not exclude clean slaughter from the public view: he would have accepted that the stabbing of Julius Caesar or even the smothering of Desdemona on stage would not overly offend the most squeamish of us, but he would have approved of Shakespeare's decision to have Macbeth beheaded in the wings.

Other things may, indeed should, be enacted in full view of as many people as possible. In 1953 the then Dean of Westminster, describing the ritual of the forthcoming coronation, told how by partaking of Holy Communion during the service, the Queen would present herself to be "a reasonable, holy and lively sacrifice to God." He stated: "She does this *coram populo*, . . ." as it were, in the face of the congregation.

*Coram Populo* is the name of a social, raiding, PvP, and light role play guild located on the Wyrmrest Accord (Horde) server. "The Order of Celestial Dawn" is the role play (IC) component of *Coram Populo.*

**Cornucopia** *The "horn of plenty", a source of unlimited wealth*

Originally this was two words, *cornu copiæ,* referring to the horn of the goat by which Zeus was suckled. Some say the goat's name was Amalthea, others (and it did happen a long time ago) that Amalthea was the name of the animal's owner. Be that as it may, a boisterous young Zeus accidentally wrenched a horn from the goat while playing with it, a thing we all know is easily done. In contrition Zeus gave the horn to the goat's owner, promising that the horn would thenceforth be empowered as it were "to scatter plenty o'er a smiling land."

"Such a fertile imagination your father had, such a cornucopia of original ideas, and such a tragic loss he was to the construction industry when he tripped over that fork-lift truck." P. J. Dorricot, *Beyond the Nursery Slopes.*

*Cornucopia* is the name of a "Turkey for Connoisseurs" magazine.

**Cum grano salis** *With a pinch (of salt)*

The motto of the sceptic down the ages. *Cum Grano Salis* is the name of a website which is "a place to moan and grump".

Pliny in his *Naturalis Historia* listed a grain of salt as being a key ingredient in an antidote to a poison. The salt is now itself an antidote to unquestioning credulity.

"The tradition of an early British chief or king being buried in a gold coffin seems to have been curiously persistent . . . Personally, I take it *cum grano*." Ernest Bramah, "The Secret of Headland Height".

" 'Hooper's deal' is actually said to have a pulverising effect on the Balakieff layer of the cortex. Myself, I take this *cum grano salis*." Stephen Potter, *Gamesmanship*.

**Cum omnibus suis pertinenciis** *With all its appurtenances*

A legal phrase occurring frequently in old documents (*vide "inquisitio post mortem" infra*) which give in detail the bequests of property to someone, or which list the properties owned by a dead person.

**Decus et tutamen (in armis)** *A beauteous safeguard (in battle)*

*Decus et tutamen* was inscribed around the edge of the larger (gold and silver) coins of Charles II, and more recently around the edge of the English pound coin. For the former coins the inscription was indeed a safeguard, being a protection against clipping, while few in their right minds would wish to clip the present coinage. Around the edge of the Scottish pound coin, which usually bears the imprint of the thistle, is inscribed *Nemo me impune lacessit* (*q.v.*); while the Welsh coin, usually showing the leek, announces around its edge "Pleidiol wyf i'm gwlad" – "I'm loyal to my country", a line of the chorus of "Mae hen wlad fy nhadau" – "Land of my Fathers".

The "beauteous safeguard" referred to was a coat of mail "in triple woven gold", seized by Aeneas from Demoleus in single-handed combat and given later to Mnestheus as a reward not, however, for any military prowess but merely for coming second in a boat race.

*Decus et Tutamen* is the motto of the Borough of Gravesend in Kent, and of the West Essex Yeomanry, while *Decus et Tutamen in Armis* is the motto of the Feltmakers Company.

**De gustibus non est disputandum** *There is no arguing about taste*

Jeremy Taylor in "Reflections upon Ridicule" quotes this as an old Latin proverb. Robert Browning wrote a poem under the title "De gustibus . . ."

"Mrs. Knox, of Aussolas, was told that I had taken Mrs. McRory for a run in the car at one o'clock in the morning, and on hearing it said, '*De gustibus non est disputandum*'. Someone, unknown, repeated this to Mrs. McRory, and told her that it meant 'You cannot touch pitch without being disgusted'." E. Œ. Somerville and Martin Ross, *Further Adventures of an Irish R.M.*

An extended version of the proverb exists, designed perhaps to confound the critics of contemporary art: *De gustibus et coloribus non est disputandum* – "There is no arguing about taste or colours."

**Delenda est Carthago** *Carthage must be destroyed*

It maybe that a girl from Carthage had spurned Cato the Elder when he was younger (not to be confused with Cato the Younger) but for whatever reason he was very much anti-Carthage and took every opportunity to express his antipathy towards her, squeezing into each of his speeches the words *Ceterum censeo delenda est Carthago* – "In my opinion Carthage, etc."

"He was especially great in his hatred of *l'infâme Angleterre*. *Delenda est Carthago* was tattooed beneath his shirt-sleeve." W. M. Thackeray, *The Newcombes*.

*Delenda Est Hispania* is the title of a book (in Spanish) by Albert Pont subtitled "Everything that Spain Does Not Want You to Know about Catalan Independence".

**Denarius** *Penny*

In 1086 the only coin in circulation in Britain was the silver penny. "Penny", like "pfennig", is a Germanic word, but the Latin name "denarius", (shortened to "d" as in "3d" for "threepence", and in "£ s d" for "librae, solidi, denarii" i.e, pounds, shillings and pence), hung on until 1971. "Denarius", shrunk into "dinar", is still in use today in Algeria, Bahrain, Iraq, Jordan, Kuwait, Libya, Macedonia, Serbia and Tunisia. Iran also once used a dinar, one-hundredth of a rial, until inflation sent it the way of the British halfpenny.

In Marlowe's "Jew of Malta", Act 2, appears the line *Hermoso placer de los dineros* – "The lovely thrill of coins!" The language is Spanish and "dinero" is still the Spanish for "money". The equivalent Portuguese word is "dinheiro": so "denarius" has given both the Spaniards and the Portuguese the name for their whole monetary system.

*Denarius* also spawned the French "denier", a coin of little value, twelve of which were worth one sou, just as twelve British pennies were worth one shilling. Shakespeare's Richard II (Act I, scene iii) said "My dukedom to a beggarly denier". The denier was used as a measure of weight, as was the penny ("pennyweight", the weight of an old silver penny, was abbreviated to "dwt", which is now more commonly met with as an abbreviation of "dead weight tonnage"). The term "denier" is still used to measure the weight of fine thread, such as silk and nylon. E.g. 12-denier nylon stockings are made from thread which weighs 12 grams per 9000 metres.

**De novo**  *Anew, from scratch*

"If I had examined everything with the care which I would have shown had we approached the case *de novo* and had no cut-and-dried story to warp my mind, would I not then have found something more definite to go upon?" Arthur Conan Doyle, *The Adventures of Sherlock Holmes*.

In bioinformatics, *de novo* is a form of sequencing, as in "de novo peptide sequencing" which, despite first impressions, is not a form of Latin-American line-dancing but a technique used in applying statistical methods to molecular biology. "*De novo* mutation" is a genetic mutation that neither parent possessed or transmitted.

There is a widespread belief that wealthier Romans would take an emetic after a meal so as to be able to start eating all over again, but some commentators find this suggestion difficult to stomach.

**De profundis**  *Out of the depths*

In its Latin form, Psalm 130 opens: "*De profundis clamavi ad te, Domine: Domine, exaudi vocem meam*" – "Out of the depths have I cried unto thee, O Lord: Lord, hear my voice."

*De Profundis* is the name of a UK based genre-defying metal group, and the electronic metal band Professional Murder Music in

2005 released a record called *De Profundis* on Wormhole Records.

Oscar Wilde wrote an *Apologia pro sua vita* in 1905 called *De Profundis*. Both Robert Browning and Elizabeth Barrett Browning wrote poems with this same title, as also did C. S. Lewis and Garcia Lorca.

" 'Dearest Elinor,' he wrote. *'De profundis clamavi*, from the depths of this repulsive hotel bedroom, . . . I call to you.' " Aldous Huxley, *Point Counter Point*.

*De Profundis* is the motto of the Norwegian Sector of the North Sea Divers Alliance and also of the Urban District Council of Bedlington in Northumberland, in a former coal-mining area.

### Desiderata  *Things to be desired*

"This something the corporal . . . supplied by an entire new system of his own . . . as one of the great *desiderata* of my Uncle Toby's apparatus." Laurence Sterne, *Tristram Shandy*.

*Desiderata* is the title of a poem, "Go placidly . . .", written by Max Ehrmann and recorded by, *inter alios*, Richard Burton and Dave Allen.

The singular is *desideratum*. Woody Allen in his story "Retribution" describes "Connie Chasen" who, through her lewd, humid eroticism and other attractions, "was the unrivalled desideratum of each young man at the party."

### Detur digniori  *Let it be given to the more deserving*

The slogan of the meritocrats, and the justification of means testing.

"We could get but one bridle here, which, according to the maxim *detur digniori*, was appropriated to Dr. Johnson's sheltie." James Boswell, *The Journal of a Tour to the Hebrides*.

"As long as promotion cometh from any human source, . . . will not such a claim as this [*viz* fourteen hungry children to feed] hold good, in spite of all our examination tests, *detur digniori's*, and optimist tendencies?" Anthony Trollope, *Barchester Towers*.

There was a time when ladies were considered to be deserving: as the schoolboy howler has it: "A gentleman is one who gives up his seat to a lady in a public convenience."

**Dies irae, dies illa, . . .** *That day is a day of wrath, . . .*

Zephaniah warned in his Old Testament prophecy that the great day of the Lord was near, a day of wrath, of "trouble and distress", of "wasteness and desolation", and sundry other forms of discomfort and dismay.

In the thirteenth century Thomas of Celano put this idea into verse of some seventeen or more stanzas, starting with:
*"Dies iræ, dies illa, Solvet sæclum in favilla, Teste David cum Sybilla . . ."* – "In the day of wrath, in that day, man shall transmute into ashes, by the word of David with the Sybil."

For many years Celano's poem was part of the Requiem Mass for the Dead, but in 1970 it was removed from the Mass, for fear no doubt that the faithful might be disheartened by its message of despair and doom. The *Dies Irae* may now however be used *ad libitum* in the Liturgy of the Hours.

In *The Bell*, Iris Murdoch quotes the tenth verse of the poem, "the egotistical and helpless cry of the Dies Irae."

Quaerens me, sedisti lassus; / Redemisti, Crucem passus; / Tantus labor non sit cassus. – "Seeking me you sat exhausted; you redeemed (me) by suffering the Cross; let so much toil not be in vain".

W. J. Irons translated the poem as a hymn: "Day of wrath! O day of mourning, / See fulfilled the prophets' warning! / Heaven and earth to ashes turning! . . ." (*Hymns Ancient and Modern* 466.)

**Disjecta membra** *Dismembered limbs*

Ovid mentions *disjecta membra*, "scattered limbs", in his *Metamorphoses,* and Horace wrote metaphorically of *disjecti membra poetæ,* "the limbs of the dismembered poet", *viz* the remaining fragments of his work, any one or two of which selected at random would be enough to allow you to assess the poet's worth. *Disjecta membra* are the scattered fragments themselves.

Writing to his publisher, John Murray, about *Don Juan,* Byron said: "Cut me up root and branch – quarter me in the *Quarterly* – send round my *disjecti membra poetæ* like those of the Levite's concubine – . . . – but don't ask me to alter it."

"The works of Shelley lie in a confused state, like the *disjecta membra* of the poet of our boyhood. They are in the strictest sense 'remains'." W. Bagehot, *Literary Essays,* "Percy Bysshe Shelley".

The phrase can be used literally: "I can hardly see what use the *disjecta membra* of my late acquaintance [*viz* the bones of a goose] are going to be to me." Sir Arthur Conan Doyle, *The Adventures of Sherlock Holmes* – "The Adventure of the Blue Carbuncle".

**Domus et placens uxor** *A home and a pleasing wife, a sweet wife*

According to Horace we (men) must leave behind three particular things when death snatches us away: *tellus et domus et placens uxor* – "the world and home and a pleasing wife".

In his *Enemies of Promise*, Cyril Connolly reflects on the fate of a friend, Godfrey Meynell, killed in action in Waziristan, gaining by his bravery a posthumous Victoria Cross, but *linquenda tellus et domus et placens uxor* – "having to leave the world and home and a loving wife". (*Linquenda* is literally "things which must be left behind or *relinquished*" and comes from the same stable as *addenda, agenda, corrigenda, pudenda* and *videnda*.)

Less tragically and less finally: "The Colonel was not so depressed as some mortals would be, who, quitting a palace and a *placens uxor*, find themselves barred into a spunging-house; . . ." W. M. Thackeray, *Vanity Fair*.

**Dulce domum** *Sweet (is the sound of) home*

The title of a school song which originated at Winchester College and was set to music by John Reading who also composed the music for the hymn *Adeste Fideles* – "O come all ye faithful". The phrase also has nostalgic connotations of homecoming since *domum ire* means "to go home".

For several years "Dulcie Domum" (*alias* Sue Limb) wrote a "Bad Housekeeping" column in the *Weekend Guardian*.

*Dulce Domum Llc* is the name of a Domestic Limited Liability Company based in Wilton, Connecticut.

**Dulce est desipere in loco**  *It is pleasant to let one's hair down on the right occasions*

Horace suggests that a bit of silliness mixed in with business discussion oils the wheels of negotiation.  The twentieth century clearly did not invent corporate hospitality.

"You haughty Southerners little know how a jolly Scotch gentleman can *desipere in loco*, and how he chirrups over his honest cups." W. M. Thackeray, *The Newcomes*.

**Dum spiro spero**  *While I have breath I have hope*

For centuries this defiant motto has dropped from the lips of members of the MacLennan clan, and has also been adopted in the course of time by several dozen prominent families, including those of Bannatyne of Newhall, Coryton of Pentillic Castle, and Jackson of Putney Hill.  It is also the motto of St. Andrews in Scotland.  In 1776 the line "*Dum spiro, spero*" was incorporated into the Great Seal of the state of South Carolina, and it is also the proud boast of the Kingdom of Sarawak.

The variant "Dum Spiro Agnew" (Spiro who?) is not attested, but surely someone must at least have muttered the phrase during the reign of Mr. Agnew as U. S. Vice-President from 1969 to 1973.

**Elixir vitae**  *The elixir of life*

In 2003 the rock band *Low Flying Owls* made its national album debut on Stinky Records with *Elixir Vitae*.

The alchemists strove hard for centuries to find the "elixir of life", a substance which, to whomever partook of it, would grant immortality, or at least an extension to one's allotted span.  (Many people during those centuries found a good enough substitute: one essential ingredient of any effective elixir was reckoned to be alcohol from one source or another.)

The word *elixir* is not originally Latin but derives from the Arabic for a curative powder to sprinkle on wounds.

A Mr. Ralph Schauss of Wyoming gave the name "Elixir Vitae" to a thick purple-coloured herbal mixture which he claimed was a cure for cancer, a cure which does not yet seem to have been widely taken up.

**E pluribus unum** *From many (comes) the one*

The phrase *E pluribus unum* was adapted from one used by Virgil, *E pluribus unus*. *E pluribus unum* was the motto of the United States of America from 1782 until 1956, when it was replaced by "In God We Trust". Whether the motto meant that many individual states combined to form the Union, or that millions of people from all over the world came together as "America", might be open to discussion.

The beckoning lines below are part of a sonnet (1883) by Emma Lazarus and they appear on a plaque in the reception hall at John F. Kennedy Airport. The whole sonnet of 14 lines appears on a plaque inside the pedestal of the Statue of Liberty.

> ". . . Give me your tired, your poor,
> Your huddled masses, yearning to breathe free;
> The wretched refuse of your teeming shore.
> Send these, the homeless, tempest-tost, to me.
> I lift my lamp beside the golden door."

"E pluribus unum" is at the time of writing the heading given to a weekly puzzle in *The Guardian* in which the letters of two or more words have to be reassembled to make a single word. *Unum e pluribus* was the motto of Wokingham Rural District Council.

Several variants on this motto exist. *E duobus unum* – "One from two" – is the motto of the Welding Institute, and also of the Corinthian Casuals Football Club, formed in 1939 by the amalgamation of the Corinthians and the Casuals football clubs. *E tribus unum* – "One from three" – is the motto of the Norfolk Joint Police Authority.

**Errare est humanum** *It is human to err*

Seneca the Younger, quoting this phrase in *Naturales Quaestiones*, merely repeats a widely used Latin proverb, which continues *perseverare diabolicum* – "to persist is of the devil". Alexander Pope extended its scope in a different direction in "An Essay on Criticism", line 525: "To err is human, to forgive, divine".

" 'I,' said Peppone, . . . 'have made one mistake in my life. I tied crackers to the clappers of your bells. It should have been half a ton of dynamite.' *'Errare humanum est,'* remarked Don Camillo." Giovanni Guareschi, *The Little World of Don Camillo.*

**Est modus in rebus** *There is a measure (or mean or middle course) in everything*

*Est modus in rebus*, translated as "There is measure in all things", is the motto of the Royal Institute of Chartered Surveyors.

**Et in Arcadia ego** *I too [have lived] in Arcadia*

The words *Et in Arcadia ego* appear on the tomb in Poussin's painting of "The Arcadian Shepherds", as well as in paintings by Guercino and Bartolomeo Schidoni. An alternative reading is: "Even in Arcady will you find me [*sc.* Death]".

Evelyn Waugh gives the heading *Et in Arcadia ego* to the first part of *Brideshead Revisited*, in which we meet a table decoration in the form of a human skull which "bore the motto '*Et in Arcadia ego*' inscribed on its forehead."

Arcadia was a district of the Peloponnesus inhabited largely by shepherds and other rustics: according to Virgil it was an area noted for its pastoral simplicity and happiness. Clearly it was the ideal place in which to live, or at least in which to have a second home.

Robert Louis Stevenson wrote a poem called *Et tu in Arcadia vixisti* – "You too have lived in Arcadia".

**Ex Africa semper aliquid novi** *There is always something new out of Africa*

Africa is a big place and has always been regarded by Europe as an inexhaustible Santa's grotto of novelties. *Ex Africa semper aliquid novi* is a proverb derived from Livy, but the profusion of curiosities coming from Africa was remarked on by Aristotle. The South African Museum adopted the motto *Semper aliquid novi Africa affert* or "Africa is always producing something new".

The announcement *Ex Africa semper aliquid novi* appears prominently on the wine boxes shipped out by the South African Vergelegen vineyard. It seems not unreasonable to suppose that Karen Blixen found in this quotation the title for her *magnum opus*, *Out of Africa*.

*Semper aliquid novi* is the motto of the Commission for the New Towns.

**Excelsior**  *Higher*

This is both the motto of New York State and the title of a poem by Longfellow in which the protagonist, carrying a banner with the strange device, "Excelsior", climbs ever higher and higher in the Alps to be found eventually by a faithful hound, though not surprisingly frozen to death. "Excelsior" is also the name of the wood shavings used to stuff, *inter alia*, teddy bears, and research needs to be done to discover whether the thriving economy of New York State was based on the teddy-bear-stuffing industry or not: and if so, whether the state motto gave its name to the teddy-bear-stuffing or *vice versa*.

" 'All right, but don't encourage him, you're always urging him to go on, *avanti, avanti, excelsior, excelsior*.' " Iris Murdoch, *The Message to the Planet*. ("*Avànti*" is Italian – "Forward!")

Luigi Manzotti's ballet *Excelsior* staged in Italy in 1881 had a cast of 600, including twelve horses, two cows and an elephant.

(N.B. *Excelsior* is higher even that *in excelsis.*)

**Exceptis excipiendis**  *With proper exceptions*

A phrase used to cover one's back when making all-inclusive statements.

"Goodness is naught unless it tends towards old age and sufficiency of means. I speak broadly and *exceptis excipiendis*." Samuel Butler, *The Way of All Flesh*.

" '. . . Two masses daily, morning and evening, primes, noons, and vespers, *aves, credos, paters* –'
'Excepting moonlight nights, when the venison is in season,' said his guest.
'*Exceptis excipiendis*,' replied the hermit." Sir Walter Scott, *Ivanhoe*.

**Exeunt omnes**  *They (all) go out*

A common stage direction. *Exeunt* is the plural of *exit*.

**Ex gratia**  *By kindness*

The victim of a mishap may have no legal claim whatsoever for damages against the author of the mishap. The latter may nonetheless, purely out of the goodness of his heart, or for other hidden motives, make an *ex gratia* payment in compensation to the victim, without thereby admitting any liability.

Curiously, no music group world wide seems to have chosen *Ex Gratia* as its title. "Excrement", yes (twice): *Ex Gratia*, no.

**Ex nihilo nihil fit**  *Nothing comes of nothing*

This is the essence of a statement of Lucretius in *De Rerum Natura*: *Nil posse creari de nilo* – "Nothing can be created out of nothing".

Karen Armstrong in *A Short History of Myth* says that the poem *Enuma Elish* begins with a theogony that shows how the gods themselves first came into being. "There is no creation *ex nihilo* but an evolutionary process. . . ."

**Ex voto**  *In consequence of a vow*

The heading of a poem by Swinburne: "When their last hour shall rise. . . ."

Jonathan Jones, writing in *The Guardian Weekend*, described the little congregation huddled in front of the marble tabernacle "with its silver treasures, ex-voto offerings, and smoky candles".

*Ex-voto* is the name of an original American deathrock band.

**Facilis descensus Averno;**
    **Noctes atque dies patet atri janua Ditis:**
    **Sed revocare gradum superasque evadere ad auras,**
    **Hoc opus, hic labor est.**
*The descent is easy to Avernus;*
    *Night and day stands wide the portal of black Dis:*
    *But then to retrace your steps and regain the light of day,*
    *This is true toil, this is labour indeed.*

Aeneas is keen to visit the shade of his dead father Anchises in the Underworld, and the Sybil here is warning him of the difficulties of making the return trip.

Rixi Marcus, writing on Bridge for *The Guardian* a little while before her death, used bits of this quotation as a commentary on successive stages in the bidding and playing of a disastrous hand. The response to an opening bid elicited *Facilis descensus Averno*; the final slam contract was marked with *Noctes atque dies,* and the actual play was prefaced by *Sed revocare gradum . . .*

(Occasionally the first line of this quotation appears as *Facilis descensus Averni*, but *Averno* is to be preferred for grammatical reasons to *Averni*. Neverthless *Facilis descensus Averni* is the name of a Black Metal band from Russia.)

"It is all very well to talk about the *facilis descensus Averni*; but in all kinds of climbing, as Catalani said of singing, it is far more easy to get up than to come down." Edgar Allan Poe, "The Purloined Letter".

*Hoc opus est* was the motto of Pedro the Cruel of Castile and Leon (*fl. c.* 1360).

### Facsimile *Make the same*

"Facsimile" started life as a hyphenated word, "fac-simile", a term applied to an exact copy of handwriting, or of a coin or similar object. The "facsimile transmission" of documents electronically is now known simply as "fax".

### Fatigatus et aegrotus *Tired and sick*

Or just plain "sick and tired".

"A wife who can behave irreproachably when her husband is by his own confession *fatigatus et ægrotus* of her, must be . . . 'either a goddess or a beastess'; and poor Elizabeth . . . Sterne appears to have been a very human creature." G. Saintsbury, Introduction to Everyman edition of Laurence Sterne, *A Sentimental Journey*.

(Saintsbury's "either a goddess or a beastess" echoes a Greek phrase from Aristotle's *Politics*: η θηριον η θεος – "e therion e theos" – "either a beast or a god".) *Vide "aegrotat" supra.*

### Fauna *Wildlife*

*Exceptis excipiendis*, any piece of wildlife that runs, flies, swims or creeps is part of the fauna of a region. If it has roots and more or less stays *in situ*, then it is more likely to be part of the flora (*q.v. infra*) of the same region.

"Fauna" in Latin was a tutelary deity or guardian god of shepherds. The word has settled into English as "faun", and into French as "faune", as in "L'après-midi d'un".

"She was named Flora, but one time in the Mission a gentleman bum . . . said, 'Flora, you seem more like a fauna-type to me.'

'Say, I like that,' she said. 'Mind if I keep it?' And she did. She was Fauna ever afterward." John Steinbeck, *Sweet Thursday*.

The narrator in Umberto Eco's *Foucault's Pendulum* remarks that on returning after a long absence to a former haunt, he felt he was on foreign soil. "The billiard table was still there, . . . , but the young fauna had changed."

"Charismatic megafauna" include the elephant, the giant panda and the blue whale.

**Favete linguis** *Be favourable to your tongues*

Horace here is appealing for a bit of quiet, asking his audience to say nothing inappropriate to the (sacred) occasion. Since the best way for them to do this was to give their tongues a rest, the phrase was equivalent to a polite request for silence.

"My good friends, *favete linguis* – To give you information, I must first . . . be possessed of it myself; and, therefore, with your leaves, I will retire into the library to examine these papers." Sir Walter Scott, *The Antiquary*.

In *Winnie Ille Pu*, the Latin version of *Winnie-the-Pooh*, Alexander Lenard translates Rabbit's "Now don't talk while I think" as "*Nunc, dum cogito, favete linguis.*"

**Feliciter audax** *Happily daring*

The word "happy" is one with many shades of meaning, and here it means "fortunate" rather than "cheerful" or "carefree". Coleridge in his "Notes on Shakespeare" uses the phrase to epitomise the style in which *Anthony and Cleopatra* is written, and it seems that his opinion is now generally accepted. "*Feliciter audax* is the motto for *Anthony and Cleopatra's* style compared with the style of Shakespeare's other works, even as it is the general motto of all his works compared with those of other poets." In the next sentence Coleridge speaks of "this happy valiancy of style".

In using this phrase Coleridge may well have had in mind the judgment of Quintilian when writing of Horace in *De Institutione Oratoria*: . . . *verbis felicissime audax*, "a most happy daring in writing".

**Felix qui potuit rerum cognoscere causas**  *Happy is he who has been able to find out the causes of things*

Because knowledge helps dispel fear of the unknown, even though it may *per contra* be offset by heightened fear of the known.

I am an *alumnus* of the London School of Economics, whose motto is *Rerum cognoscere causas*.  The college was always among the *avant-garde* (*acies prima*) of its day, an *arbiter elegantiarum* especially in ladies' fashion, and before the Second World War it was known to its sister colleges of London University as:

> "*Rerum cognoscere causas*,
> The place where women wear trousers."

The LSE shares its motto with Sheffield University and with Humberside Collegiate Institute located in Toronto, Canada.

*Felix qui potuit* is the motto of Sir William Carew of Devon, and *Rerum cognoscere causas* is also the motto of the Institute of Brewing, with hints of mystery ingredients in beer. (Sometimes it is better perhaps not to know what you are drinking.)

### Feræ Naturæ  *Of a wild nature*

Sometimes used to mean just "wild animals".

"Or were pheasants *feræ naturæ*, under no one's control, like the snails thrown over the garden fence in A. P. Herbert's classic Misleading Case, 'Is a snail a wild animal?' "     Katherine Whitehorn, writing in *The Observer*.

Just for the record and solely by way of illustration and with no malice aforethought on my part, I note that Dryden in "The Mock Astrologer" avers that "women are not comprised in our Laws of Friendship: they are *Feræ Naturæ*."

### Festina lente  *Hasten slowly*

This is a direct ancestor of our "More haste, less speed", and advises caution rather than procrastination.  It was a favourite both of Erasmus, and, in its Greek form, *Σπευδε βραδεως*, "*speude bradeos*", of Augustus Caesar.

> Lord Chancellor:     Recollect yourself, I pray,
>                 And be careful what you say –
>                     As the ancient Romans said, *festina lente*, . . .
>     W. S. Gilbert, *Iolanthe*, Act 1

The Festina Lente Foundation, based at Bray in Hampshire, offers training in equestrianism and horticulture, both of these being skills which presumably cannot be mastered in a hurry.

*Festina lente* is the motto of a number of families including those of Colquhon, Dunsany and the Earls of Onslow, and also of Audenshaw Urban District Council in Lancashire.

## Fiat *Let it be*

In *Villette*, Charlotte Bronte speaks ruefully of blanks in her heroine's life, "the result of circumstances, the fiat of fate, a part of my life's lot. . . ."

"My grandmother's fiats, delivered in staccato tones of an awful majesty, earned her, among us devotees of Rider Haggard, the soubriquet of "Ayesha", "She who must be obeyed." P. J. Dorricot, *Nursery Tales.*

## Fiat lux *Let there be light*

"And God said, Let there be light: and there was light." Genesis, i. 3.

*Fiat lux* is an understandably popular title both with film-makers and with firms producing lighting equipment. It is the motto of the Moorfields Eye Hospital in London.

## Flora *The goddess of flowers*

Flora Poste was the heroine of Stella Gibbons' *Cold Comfort Farm*, but her busy life was tranquil compared with that of the original Flora, the Roman goddess of flowers. The latter started life as a nymph, Chloris, who having been ravished by her brother Zephyr, the spring breeze, was thereby disqualified from continuing as a nymph. However all ended well, as she was swiftly transmuted into the goddess. The whole episode is presented by Botticelli on the right hand side of his painting *La Primavera* ("Spring").

> "O, for a draught of vintage! that hath been
> Cool'd a long time in the deep-delved earth,
> Tasting of Flora and the country green. . . ."
> John Keats, "Ode to a Nightingale".

"Flora" is the term used to denote the plant life of a region. *Cf. "fauna" supra.*

**Fons et origo**  *The source and origin*

Literally *fons* is a spring or fountain.  *Fons et Origo* is the motto of the La Fontaine family.

" . . . you have the privilege of knowing one of the most complete young blackguards about town, and the *fons et origo* of the whole trouble." E. W. Hornung, *Raffles*.

"The *fons et origo* of this view [that a woman should not resist attack by a man] seems to be Chief Inspector B-. H-." John Naughton, writing in *The Observer*.

"I'm being good.  I am aping the *fons et origo* of domestic virtue.  If we had twins I'd call them Lares and Penates (*qq.v.*)." Julian Barnes, *Talking It Over*.

**Fragrat post funera virtus**  *Virtue smells sweet after death*

Virtue is one of the few things that do.

> "The glories of our blood and state
> Are shadows, not substantial things; . . .
> Only the actions of the just
> Smell sweet and blossom in the dust."
>     James Shirley.

*Fragrat post funera virtus* is the motto of the Chiesly family.

**Gaudeamus igitur, juvenes dum sumus**  *Let us rejoice therefore, while we are still young*

The opening words of a song which I found first in *The Scottish Students' Songbook*, and which has been sung by students throughout Europe over the centuries.  It also has the title *De Brevitate Vitae* – "On the Shortness of Life".  It is set to music composed *c*. A.D. 1267 by Strada, Bishop of Bologna.  Brahms quotes the tune in his *Academic Festival Overture*.

It is sadly unlikely that this phrase gave birth to the term "Gaudy", an often rowdy entertainment at certain universities, but the verb "*gaudire*" – "to rejoice" – is the common source of the two "g" words.

**Gratias tibi agimus**  *We give thee thanks*

These were the opening words of a prayer recited at lunch-time at my grammar school.  The prayer went on to thank God for all his blessings, among which we were encouraged to think was whatever was about to appear on our plates.  Very often after the meal we could sympathise with the small girl whose grace after meat was simply "Thank God I wasn't sick".  *Cf. "Pabulum" infra.*

**Habeas corpus**  *You have the body*

If you are so careless as to be arrested on a serious charge and detained in custody, a writ of *habeas corpus* [*ad subjuciendum*] requires the police or any other arresting authority to bring you before a magistrate, who will then decide whether you should remain in detention or be released.  The Latin is in the present subjunctive, but has the impact of an imperative: "You are to produce the body".

"The time of the assizes soon came, and I was removed by *habeas corpus* to Oxford, where I expected certain conviction and condemnation; . . ." Henry Fielding, *Tom Jones.*

"Colonel Samuel B. Venus's ever-loving wife is not present in her boudoir at this hour, and neither is Colonel Samuel B. Venus, and in fact I afterward learn that the only way Colonel Samuel B. Venus can get in there is on a writ of habeas corpus." Damon Runyon, "Cemetery Bait".

**Hic haec hoc**  *This, this, this*

Someone c. 1600 wrote a brief humorous poem which began "Hic, hoc, the carrion crow".

*Hic* means "this" but only if "this" is masculine.  If it's feminine, then it's *haec*, but if it falls somewhere between the two it's *hoc*. Technically, *hoc* is neuter, which is a Latin compound word *ne + uter* meaning "not either".  The next line in the pattern is *hunc hanc hoc*, but enough is enough for the moment.

**Hinc illae lacrimae**  *Hence those tears*

Terence used these words in his play "Andria", but the phrase was commonly used in other works to mean: "So that's what the fuss was really about!"

"Enrapture – *Hinc Illae Lacrimae*" is the title of the first track of the album *Domus Mundi* (Home of the World) by the Austrian symphonic black metal band Hollenthon.

"I am too much addicted to the study of philosophy; *hinc illæ lacrymæ*, sir, that's my misfortune. Too much learning hath been my ruin." Henry Fielding, *Tom Jones*.

Edgar Allan Poe in "The Mystery of Marie Rogêt" adapts the phrase to *Et hinc illae irae?* or "And hence that anger?"

"Were Freud right and sex supreme, we should live almost in Eden. Alas, only half right. Adler also half right. *Hinc illae lac.*" Aldous Huxley, *Eyeless in Gaza*.

### Humanum est errare *It is human to err*

Merely another way of saying "*Errare est humanum*" *q.v. supra*.

### Impedimenta *Encumbrances, impediments*

*Impedimenta* is a word now firmly associated with holiday makers. It is the plural of *impedimentum*, "a hindrance". In Roman times it referred to the baggage and essential supplies carried by its armies, the transporting of which slowed down the armies' speed of advance and impeded their progress. (Research needs to be done into the extent to which the Roman definition of "baggage" embraced camp-followers.)

In J. K. Rowling's *Harry Potter*, the powerful spell *Impedimenta*, comprising the Impediment Jinx and the Impediment Curse, is capable of "tripping, freezing, binding, knocking back and generally impeding the target's progress towards the caster".

### In absentia *In one's absence*

*In Absentia* are fully defined as an instrumental jazz fusion hardcore metal band.

Writing in *The Observer* R. Bruce Lockhart said: "Higgs was sentenced to death *in absentia*, along with my father and Reilly."

The concept of *in-absentia* health care seems to have started with the second century Roman physician Galen. You sent him a letter describing your symptoms: he would diagnose your disease and by return post would prescribe the appropriate treatment. Today the same package is available on-line.

**In articulo mortis** *At the point of death, in the arms of death*

"As to the youthful sufferer, he weathered each storm like a hero. Five times was that youth 'in articulo mortis', and five times did he miraculously survive." Charlotte Brontë, *Villette*.

Sometimes written (for the sake of easier scansion) as *Mortis in articulo*. In his poem "The Song Against Grocers", which begins "God made the wicked Grocer . . .", G. K. Chesterton writes:

> "The evil-hearted Grocer
> Would call his mother 'Ma'am',
> And bow at her and bob at her
> Her aged soul to damn,
> And rub his horrid hands and ask
> What article was next,
> Though *mortis in articulo*
> Should be her proper text."

In *Epistolæ ad Quintum Fratrem*, V, 19, Cicero says *in ipso articulo temporis* – "at this point in time". Perhaps not surprisingly there appears to be no phrase in Latin for "at this moment in time".

**In flagrante delicto** *In the act*

Usually in the act of (illicit) love. The Latin has the implication of a "blazing crime" being committed at the time.

"The number of times my cousin Jethro was caught *in flagrante delicto* earned him the title of 'The Lothario of Bishop's Stortford'." P. J. Dorricot, *Beyond the Nursery Slopes*.

In William Golding's *Close Quarters*, a character suggests that, had little Marion not detained her "uncle", he would have been "a devil of a sight nearer being detected *in flagrante delicto* than I was!"

" 'Unfortunately for Kemp, however, Cedric Downes discovered the guilty pair *in flagrante delicto*, which as you will remember, Lewis, is the Latin for having your pants down.' " Colin Dexter, *The Jewel that was Ours*.

**In loco parentis** *In place of a parent*

One drawback of being a teacher is constantly having other people's children under your feet. Being *in loco parentis* one is entrusted with their care and is adjured to treat them as a loving parent would, but one is usually very glad to return them to the care of their true loving parent(s) at the end of the school day.

" 'And why, Colonel Newcombe,' Virtue exclaimed, laying a pudgy little hand on its heart – 'why did I treat Clive so? Because I stood towards him *in loco parentis*; because he was as a child to me and I to him as a mother.' " W. M. Thackeray, *The Newcombes*.

*In Loco Parentis* is the motto of Cheadle Hulme School, Cheshire, and also somewhat unexpectedly of 200 Squadron of the R.A.F.

**In medias res** *Into the thick of things*

Horace was irritated by Homer's habit of plunging the reader into the middle of a story, assuming that the reader already knows or can somehow divine telepathically what went before.

Writing of C. S. Lewis's novels in *The Guardian*, John Mullan remarked that at the start of *The Voyage of the Dawn Treader*, Edmund, Lucy and Eustace find themselves simply plunged into the sea near King Caspian's ship. "*In medias res* is how most of the novels begin, with children hurried into a story that has already begun."

*In Medias Res* is the motto of 258 Squadron of the R.A.F., while *Silenter in Medias Res* – "Silently into the thick of things" – is the motto of 177 Squadron of the R.A.F.

There is a good argument to be made for using certain Latin phrases rather than their equivalent English ones, on the grounds that the Latin is dispassionate and not loaded with connotations. *In medias res* is a case in point. "Into the thick of things" brings with it a suggestion of "hurly-burly" whereas *in medias res* is a simple statement that we are entering without fuss into a situation which is already partly developed.

(*Cf. "ab initio"*, *"ab incunabulo"* and *"ab ovo" supra.*)

**In situ** *In place*

To an archaeologist, an artefact is *in situ* if it has not been moved from the place where its last owner dropped it, given that this happened long enough ago. The notion can be applied to any object which has been gathering dust in a particular spot for some time.

According to a newspaper report, "the most popular form of laser eye surgery is 'laser-assisted in-situ keratomileusis' or Lasik for short." The inclusion of "in-situ" is intriguing – one wonders if the "non-in-situ" or "ex-situ" treatment involves taking the eye out, doing the necessary, and then popping it back in again. The mind (or the mind's eye) boggles.

"When we came to fumigate her room, Aunt Enid refused to budge, so we were forced to go ahead with the old lady *in situ.*" P. J. Dorricot, *Beyond the Nursery Slopes.*

**In statu pupillari** *In the position of a ward*

This is the complement of *in loco parentis*, *q.v. supra*. The implication is whoever is *in loco parentis* needs to keep a close eye on whoever is *in statu pupillari*.

"Philip had a joke about his wife's housekeeping which perhaps may apply to other young women who are kept by over-watchful mothers too much *in statu pupillari.*" W. M. Thackeray, *The Adventures of Philip.*

Julian Barnes in *Talking It Over* admits he could not quite remember the identities of the people under consideration but that were those currently "*in statu pupillare (sic)* to be assembled in a *décontractée* atmosphere − rather like, say, a police line-up", he felt that the whole matter could be discussed.

**Integer vitae scelerisque purus** *(He who is) blameless in respect to his life, and has no share in wickedness (need not carry spears, poisoned arrows, etc)*

Horace, taking a stroll in the local woods and having left his bow and arrows at home, met a monstrous wolf which sloped off without harming him, having assessed him as *Integer vitae scelerisque purus* – or at least so Horace modestly claimed.

"Who so *integer vitæ scelerisque purus,* it was asked, as Mr. Pontifex of Battersby?" Samuel Butler, *The Way of all Flesh.*

John Quincy Adams, sixth President of the U.S.A., dedicated his translation of Horace's ode to a certain Sally:

> The man in righteousness arrayed,
>      A pure and blameless liver, . . .

where the "liver" is to be interpreted as in "exister" rather than as in "kidneys".

*Integer vitæ* is the motto of the Christie family of Glyndebourne.

**In toto** *In total, altogether*

"He asked leave, therefore, to withdraw the charge *in toto* . . ." R. Kipling, "The Village that Voted the Earth was Flat".

"The chairs are upholstered in a material of bottle-green; and the colour combination of the room *in toto* has appealed to many . . . as an unusually happy one." Colin Dexter, *The Remorseful Day*.

"In-toto Kitchens" is a firm specialising in supplying complete kitchens, while "in toto theatre", offering a total theatre experience, is based in London.

"Toto" is the name of Dorothy's dog in *The Wizard of Oz*, and it has been suggested that his name derives from the fact that he loves Dorothy completely, i.e. *in toto*.

**In transitu** *In transit*

The final "u" of this phrase dropped off almost imperceptibly at some time in the past, so that the phrase "in transit" (more usually encountered as "goods in transit" or "lost in transit") is now accepted as being entirely English. It is nevertheless derived immediately from the Latin.

If a supplier suddenly has reason to believe that goods he has sent away are not likely to be paid for, the law of "Stoppage in transitu" allows him to seize those goods while they are still in transit.

**In vacuo** *In a vacuum*

"The fault of [this speculative and indeterminate kind of study] is sometimes to produce a sort of lecturer *in vacuo*, ignorant of exact pursuits, and diffusive of vague words." W. Bagehot, "The First Edinburgh Reviewers".

"It is one thing to discuss *in vacuo* whether So-and-so will join us tonight, and another when So-and-So's honour is pledged to come . . ." C. S. Lewis, "On Obstinacy in Belief".

The phrase is also used literally. The M.E.I. Students' Handbook lists the symbol C (= 2.998 x $10^8$ m s$^{-1}$) as representing the speed of light *in vacuo*.

**In vinculis matrimonii** *In the bonds of marriage*

Aubrey Anon, writing in *The Guardian*, pointed out that Sir Alan Herbert in his Matrimonial Causes Act of 1937, making divorce much more widely and easily available than hitherto, took on "bishops who tried to keep married couples *in vinculis*" (i.e. married).

The *vinculum matrimonii* is the marriage bond, and *a vinculo matrimonii* means "from the bond of matrimony". (*In vinculis* is in fact plural, and any married person knows the many and various bonds which tie a happy couple together.)

In mathematics, a *vinculum* is a horizontal line used in place of brackets: Newton used *vincula* rather than brackets in his mathematical writings. The vinculum survives today in the square root sign, so that $\sqrt{3^2 + 4^2}$ (= 5) is not the same as $\sqrt{3^2} + 4^2$ (= 19).

The fraction bar also acts as a *vinculum* and when we remove a fraction bar in a mathematical equation, we must often replace it with brackets. For example, if we simplify:

$$x = \frac{3}{x} - \frac{x-2}{x}$$

by multiplying both sides of the equation by $x$, we must write $x^2 = 3 - (x - 2)$ as the next step in the solution.

On the London Embankment stands a memorial to its builder Sir Joseph Bazalgette. It reads *Vincula flumini posuit,* which states that "He set bounds to the river" or simply that "He bound the river".

**Ius primae noctis** *The right of the first night*

The French *Droit de Seigneur* included *inter alia* the alleged right of the feudal lord to spend the first night of a vassal's marriage with his (*sc.* the vassal's) wife. Sadly (or happily – for the vassals if not for their wives), there seems to be no firm evidence that such a practice ever existed. Nevertheless those who dream they were a seigneur in a previous incarnation may continue to dream.

George Orwell in *Nineteen Eighty-four* reports that there was also something called the *jus primae noctis*, which would probably not be mentioned in a textbook for children. "It was the law by which every capitalist had the right to sleep with any woman working in one of his factories."

The "first night" need not be a nuptial one. In "Two or Three Graces", Aldous Huxley notes that to simple mortals, forced to pay for their pleasures, the sight of a free ticket is always impressive. "The critic's *jus primae noctis* seems to them an enviable thing."

**Laborare est orare (*or* orare est laborare)** *To work is to pray (work is prayer)*

*Laborare est orare* was the motto of the Benedictine monks who were supposed to fill all the hours of the day with useful work (or prayer). It is the motto also of Gloucester Training College and of the London Borough of Willesden, and it is the title of a painting by John Roger Herbert (1810–1890) now in the Tate Gallery.

"But he was damned if he'd do anything. Work, the gospel of work, the sanctity of work, *laborare est orare*, – all that tripe and nonsense." Aldous Huxley, *Point Counter Point*.

" 'The world has gone well with you, I am glad to hear and see.' '*Qui laborat, orat* [Who works, prays],' said Hatton in a silvery voice, 'is the gracious maxim of our Holy Church, and I venture to believe my prayers and vigils have been accepted, for I have laboured in my time . . .' " Benjamin Disraeli, *Sybil*.

*Ora Et Labora* – "Pray and work" – is the name of a trawler (Z34) registered in Zeebrugge.

**Lapsus linguae** *A slip of the tongue*

"I'm sorry, darling, forgive me. When I called your mother an old *mat*, that was a *lapsus linguae*. I meant to call her an old *bat*."

"There is nothing more illiberal than the ostentatious correction of an obvious *lapsus linguae*." Patrick O'Brian, *Desolation Island*. (Illiberal or not, the temptation to correct "boomkin nottings" to "bowsprit nettings" is understandable.)

To *lapsus linguæ* we may add both *lapsus calami,* a slip of the pen, and *lapsus memoriæ,* a slip of the memory, lapses which occur as often in the young as in those in the grip of *anno domini*.

(Now that so many of us have abandoned the pen for the computer keyboard, it seems legitimate to add to the above list *lapsus digitis* – "a slip of the finger" – or *lapsus claviaturae* – " a slip of the keyboard". The Vatican has produced a lexicon of Latin words for modern artefacts and institutions, choosing *claviatura* for both the piano keyboard and the computer keyboard. The full list can be found in *Lexicon Recentis Latinitatis*, accessible through Wikipedia, "Ecclesiastical Latin".)

## Lares et penates *Household gods*

*Lares et penates* are those personal possessions which make up a "home". To the Romans *lares* were the household gods, often deified ancestors, with a guardian role, while *penates* were also deities, but with the declared function of bringing prosperity to the house, and in particular of bringing into it a regular supply of food.

"They flit from furnished room to furnished room, transients for ever – . . . they carry their *lares et penates* in a band-box. . . ." O. Henry, "The Furnished Room".

Writing in *The Guardian* of the Aga stove, Matthew Fort suggested: "In a way, the Aga has become the contemporary equivalent of the *lares et penates* – household gods – of ancient Rome . . ."

## Latet anguis in herba *A snake lurks in the grass*

It may be confidently assumed that the said snake lurks for no benevolent purpose, whence the pejorative flavour of the phrase "a snake in the grass".

"Latet Anguis In Herba" is a Harry Potter fanfic story written by Slide.

## Locus classicus *The stock example, the classic example*

"Our *locus classicus* [of the 'second wife' kind of affair] here was Sara Keays and Cecil Parkinson." Simon Hoggart, writing in *The Observer*.

Colin Dexter, in *The Remorseful Day*, states that before she was murdered the dead woman had a client in bed with her, "and if ever there was a *locus classicus* for what they call *coitus interruptus* this was it, because someone interrupted the proceedings."

The phrase *splendide mendax* – "nobly untruthful" (*q.v. infra*) is held to be the *locus classicus* of an oxymoron; while it has been claimed that the *Huang Di Nei Jing* ("The Yellow Emperor's Inner Classic") is the *locus classicus* of Chinese medical theory and especially of acupuncture and moxibustion.

**Locus standi**  *A place for standing, a right to interfere*

*Locus standi* is also the right to bring an action or an appeal before a court.

"Before he engages in further criticism of the organisation's actions, he ought to take a very close look at his *locus standi*." Financial report.

Iris Murdoch, in *Under the Net*, seems to use the phrase to mean "status": "It's bad for one's *locus standi* to live on a woman's charity."

*Locus standi* has been proposed as the most fitting Latin translation for a "car parking space".

**Loquitur**  *Speaks*

" 'If,' he was told, 'you could be alarmed into the semblance of modesty, you would charm everybody; but remember my joke against you,' (Sydney Smith *loquitur*) . . ." W. Bagehot, "The First Edinburgh Reviewers".

Under the pseudonym of "Brunette Coleman", Philip Larkin wrote a poem called "Fourth Former *loquitur*".

*Loquitur* is a company which provides high-quality, intensive and personalised Specialised English Legal Language Courses for lawyers.

**Lustrum**  *A period of five years*

A *lustrum* was a purificatory sacrifice made on behalf of the Roman people every five years, the use of the term being extended to indicate the equivalent lapse of time. The Roman people purified themselves in the interim by frequent washing, as did our own Queen Elizabeth I, who is said to have taken a bath once a year whether she needed it or not.

"The sacred flame of curiosity burns dimmer and dimmer as lustrum is added to lustrum in human life, but it is never extinguished." "The Circus at Olympia", *Manchester Guardian,* November 1889 (*sic*).

In the film *Rooster Cogburn*, the judge tells Rooster (John Wayne) that "you have served this court for almost two lustrums".

*Lustrum* was anglicised to "lustre".  In *Roundabout Papers*,

Thackeray says: "Was there not a Lord Orville in your case too? As you think of him eleven lustres pass away." ("On a Peal of Bells".)

**Lusus naturae**  *A freak of nature*
A famous *lusus naturae* was the "vegetable lamb", said by Sir John Mandeville to be rooted to the ground by a thick stem growing from its belly.

*"Lusus naturæ"* could be a useful phrase to use when one wishes to circumvent the many restrictions on describing in pejorative terms anyone who is clearly not 100% *compos mentis*, but please note that this publication is nothing if not politically correct.

"A 'woman of intellect' it appeared, was a sort of 'lusus naturæ', a luckless accident, wanted neither as wife nor worker."  Charlotte Brontë, *Villette*.

" 'But dwarfs,' he read, 'he held in abhorrence as *lusus naturae* and of evil omen.' "  Aldous Huxley, *Chrome Yellow*.

*Lusus* is a fourth declension noun, as are *apparatus* and *casus* (*qq.v.*), and takes the ending *–us* in both the singular and the plural (nominative).  Its literal meaning is "sport" or "a game", and *lusus naturæ* is one of nature's little jokes.

**Mare nostrum**  *Our sea*
At one time the Romans had colonised the whole shoreline of the Mediterranean, and so felt entitled to refer to the Med as "Our Sea". Gabriele D'Annunzio (1863-1938) suggested reviving the title as *Il Mare Nostrum* to support the expansion of the Italian navy and to justify Italy's trying to rebuild her old empire along the sea's African shores.

The *Mare Nostrum* restaurant in Miami specialises in Mediterranean dishes.

**Matre pulchra filia pulchrior**  *Fairer daughter of a fair mother*
Horace, carried away by the superabundance of beauty before him, begins his ode by addressing the daughter rather than the mother – *O . . . filia pulchrior . . .*

"Faith, the beauty of *filia pulcrior* (*sic*) drove *pulcram* (*sic*) *matrem* out of my head! and yet as I came down the river, and thought about the pair, the pallid dignity and exquisite grace of the matron had the uppermost, and I thought her even more noble than the virgin." W. M. Thackeray, *Henry Esmond.*

## Maxima debetur puero reverentia *The utmost reverence is due to a child*

Juvenal insisted in his *Satires* that a child's innocence (whenever it can be found) must be respected at all times.

" '*Maxima debetur pueris*', says Jones (a fellow of very kind feeling . . .), and writing on his card to Hoskins, hinted to him that a boy was in the room, and a gentleman who was quite a greenhorn; hence that the songs had better be carefully selected." W. M. Thackeray, *The Newcombes.* (The speaker uses the plural *pueris*, "to children".)

## Mea culpa *Through my fault*

In the Public Confession in the Mass, the words: *Peccavi nimis cogitatione, verbo, et opere* – "I have sinned exceedingly in thought, word and deed", are followed by: *Mea culpa, mea culpa, mea maxima culpa* – "through my fault, through my fault, through my most grievous fault."

Richard Brooks wrote in *The Observer* of a former government economic adviser who suspected that his advice in the past might have helped create unemployment: "Budd's *mea culpa*, admirable in principle, may not go down so well with the jobless".

"But Oliver used to be called Nigel. *Mea culpa, mea maxima culpa.* Or rather, not. Or rather, Thanks, Mum." Julian Barnes, *Talking It Over.*

The negative of *mea culpa* is *mea non culpa* or "Don't blame me!" Gideon Haigh in *Silent Revolutions* states that "Slater's *mea non culpa* was ghosted by an Australian rock journalist, Jeff Apter", and he goes on to suggest that it read at times like one of those self-mortification showbiz memoirs, lacking only a visit to the Betty Ford Clinic.

In *The Bell*, Iris Murdoch, perhaps with St. Augustine or with the Catholic service for Holy Saturday in mind, uses the phrase *felix culpa* – "joyous fault": ". . . the joys of repentance, . . . the delicious pleasure of . . . grovelling in the dust. *O felix culpa!*"

**Media vita in morte sumus** *In the midst of life we are in death*

The burial service for the dead (not to be confused with that for the living) asserts at the graveside that "in the midst of life we are in death". In the old Latin service of the Catholic Church this is *media vita in morte sumus.*

*Media Vita in Morte Sumus* is the name of a Mass by Nicholas Gombert (*fl. c.* 1540), and also the title of a Danish horror film of 1993 directed by Nina Powers-Bates.

**Memento** *A keepsake, a reminder*

This occasionally crops up misspelled as "momento" through a failure to link it to the word "memory". It means simply "remember". *Memento mei* – "Remember me" – is the motto of the L'Estrange family.

A "memento" is now simply a reminder, perhaps of a friend or of a holiday. A *memento mori* ("remember you must die") is a stark reminder of our mortality. *Memento mori* is the motto of the Trappists and is the title of a novel by Muriel Spark. A *memento mori* often took the form of a skull or skulls on the border of a memorial to a dead person. *Memento mori* has no obvious plural; the phrase is used as its own plural. Dr. C. Helman writing in *The Observer Magazine*, reports that "These *memento mori* [hundreds of tiny skeletons, skulls and bones] are bought and displayed throughout Mexico on All Souls' Day. . . ."

In the midst of life we are occasionally in death. "[Bidlake] could not remember having spoken to her more than three or four times in all the quarter of a century which had turned Mary Betterton into a *memento mori*." Aldous Huxley, *Point Counter Point.*

**Mirabile dictu** *Wonderful to relate*

The phrase is used to indicate surprise, and indeed often translates as "surprise, surprise".

". . . *mirabile dictu*, there were one or two even greater duffers than I on the Abbey cricket field." E. W. Hornung, *Raffles.*

"And in any case, 5C weren't all that bad, really, and she, Julia Stevens, *mirabile dictu*, was one of the few members of staff who could handle that motley and unruly crowd." Colin Dexter, *The Daughters of Cain.*

In *The Guardian*, John Crace reported that "Stephen Fry . . . managed to casually bump into both Sting and Morgan Freeman – *mirabile dictu!* – on his potter around the US".

The reverse side of the coin is *horribile dictu* – "terrible to relate".

## Mobile perpetuum

The same as *Perpetuum mobile* (*vide infra*).

### Modus operandi (M.O.) *The way of working*

We are all creatures of habit, and the criminal is no exception. He tends to use the same methods in committing many of his crimes so that his misdemeanours may well show a regular pattern. This pattern is his *modus operandi*, and an experienced detective will often find this helps in identifying the criminal and even in making an early arrest.

"The corpse was missing a right-hand thumb, a left big toe and half an ear, and the words 'Watford United' had been carved on its stomach *post mortem,* possibly with a blunt Stanley knife. It did not take Detective Superintendent Cartwright long to recognise the *modus operandi* of the East Basingstoke serial killer." Q. Q. Enwright, *Mistress and Maid.*

It is not only the criminal classes who enjoy an M.O. Anita Brookner in *Altered States* speaks of her fascination with a woman "whose characteristics and whose *modus operandi* were precisely the opposite of those which delineated Angela."

The plural of *modus* is *modi*. "I sit at the piano, . . . , and we adopt one of our three *modi operandi*." David Mitchell, *Cloud Atlas.*

The phrase can also be used impersonally. Joanna Slaughter, writing in *The Observer* of the Access fund to help students with no money, said: ". . . the arithmetic of this exercise has always been suspect and its *modus operandi* appears close to disastrous."

### Modus vivendi *A way of living (together)*

*Modus Vivendi* is the name of a Greek firm making men's underwear.

Any two (or more) people, each with personal preferences and prejudices, who choose to live together, have to be prepared to make compromises if they want to avoid domestic bloodshed. In short, they establish (with luck) a *modus vivendi*. Any two or more political parties attempting to form a coalition have to sink their differences and establish a common ground: they too have to find a *modus vivendi*.

"It was not exactly that he had pressed and she had invited. They had simply simultaneously discovered a relaxed and cheerful *modus vivendi* together." Iris Murdoch, *The Message to the Planet*.

However, the phrase has been used in a different sense. In Colin Dexter's *The Remorseful Day*, we read of Morse's "resumption of his erstwhile *modus vivendi*", making the phrase synonymous with "life style".

## Mons Veneris *The Mount of Venus*

The human (female) body sports three Mounts of Venus: two, sitting one at the base of each thumb, are fairly boring, while the third, a fatty elevation on the pubic symphysis, is more exciting.

*Mons Veneris* is the name of a Portuguese Black Metal band.

*Mons Veneris* became "Venusberg" in German, and although presumably still a mountain of sorts, was the subterranean home of Venus. Tannhäuser found his way to Venusberg and spent a year there worshipping the goddess.

" 'People will insist,' [Mary] used to say, 'on treating the *mons Veneris* as though it were Mount Everest. Too silly.' " Aldous Huxley, *Eyeless in Gaza*.

(*Cf. "Pervigilium Veneris" infra.*)

## Multum in parvo *Much in a small space*

An example which may or may not come to mind is a Swiss Army penknife. *Multum in Parvo* was the name of a compact lawn mower made by the firm of Green in the 1880's. *Multum in Parvo* is also the motto of Rutland, the smallest county in England (smallest except at high tide when the Isle of Wight is marginally smaller).

A bronze sculpture of a pug dog by Louise Peterson has the title *Multum in Parvo*. The Connecticut firm of Pugsplace offer items of clothing such as a "*Multum in Parvo* Pug Hoodie" for humans and a "*Multum in Parvo* tee-shirt" for dogs.

O. Henry, in "The Hand that Riles the World", speaks of "a combination steak-beater, shoe-horn, marcel-waver, monkey wrench, nail file, potato masher and Multum in Parvo tuning fork".

**Mutatis mutandis** *With the necessary changes being made*

*Mutatis Mutandis* is the name of a "collaborative online role-playing environment" and also of a theatre company run by David Whiteley in Ottawa.

"A young girl . . . in a dark serge skirt . . . disclosing a pair of workmanlike rubber boots, which, *mutatis mutandis*, were very like those Davies was wearing." Erskine Childers, *The Riddle of the Sands*.

N. Jarrett writing in *The Observer Magazine* referred to a claim that it was no matter that a group of so-called artists had an insufficient grasp of the rules of their craft – indeed that many of them didn't really know much about painting at all. "Imagine," he said, "this observation applied, *mutatis mutandis*, to a bricklayer or an airline pilot."

And here is George Orwell in "New Words" being slightly technical about a couplet which is said to express general relief that Queen Elizabeth had got over her grand climacteric without coming to any harm. "The dictionary-meaning has, as nearly always, *something* to do with the real meaning, but not more than the 'anecdote' of a picture has to do with its design. And it is the same with prose, *mutatis mutandis*."

**Mutato nomine de te fabula narratur** *Change the name and the story applies to yourself*

This is Horace. *Mutato nomine* is an "ablative absolute" like *mutatis mutandis (supra)*, and translates as "The name having been changed". Horace prefaces the phrase with the words: *Quid rides?* – "Why do you laugh?" The listener to the tale, falling about laughing, could well himself be the butt of the joke contained therein.

The tale need not be humorous. " '*De te fabula narratur*,' I said to myself," recounts Umberto Eco in *The Name of the Rose,* and the speaker wonders if the pages did not already contain the story of future events in store for him.

**Nemo me impune lacessit** *No one provokes me with impunity*

This is the motto of the kings of Scotland and of all Scottish regiments. It is the motto of the Order of the Thistle, and also of the Nettles family, which if one thinks about it seems appropriate. The phrase is engraved around the edge of the Scottish pound coin, the coin itself bearing the impression of a thistle.

*Nemo me impune lacessit* appeared as the motto of a seal on a $20 bill issued in Georgia in 1778, although here the threat was not from a mere plant but from a rattlesnake.

*Cf. "Donat habere viro decus et tutamen. . ." supra.*

**Ne plus ultra** *No more, no further, the ultimate*

Literally "no more beyond". Many believe that Marilyn Monroe was the *ne plus ultra* of all twentieth-century pin-up girls, with Betty Grable just failing to come abreast of her.

J. Sams, writing in *The Observer,* says: "*Semiramide* is the *ne plus ultra* of *opera seria*, a great, neo-classical edifice built of everything that Rossini had learned."

The twin Pillars of Hercules, marking the westward boundary of the ancient world, were set on either side of the Straits of Gibraltar, and tradition has it that they were joined by a scroll bearing the words *Ne Plus Ultra*. A Spanish silver dollar issued in 1563 displayed the two pillars linked by such a scroll, and it is said that this design was simplified to give the familiar symbol for a dollar, $ (with two vertical lines).

**Nescit vox missa reverti** *The published word can never be recalled*

This is our old friend Horace in his *Ars Poetica* ("The Art of Poetry") advising the eldest son of *his* old friend Piso not to rush too hastily into print (or in those days, into manuscript). It means literally, "a voice sent forth knows not how to return". A safe interval between writing something down and then inflicting it on the general public, after due pruning and polishing, would be something like nine years.

*Nescit vox missa reverti* is the motto of the Halsey family.

"He was gone; and Morse knew, within a second of his going, that he would not be forgiving himself easily for such monumental

ingratitude.  But the damage was done: *nescit vox missa reverti*."
Colin Dexter, *The Wench is Dead.*

A variant of this *sententia* is *Nescit semen missum reverti*, which
fuelled the search for an effective morning-after pill.

**Ne sit ancillæ tibi amor pudori**  *Do not be ashamed of your love
for a serving-maid*

A steady supply of pretty serving-maids is a *sine qua non* of any
happy household and my regret is that my own family has never
been able to afford one, not even part-time.   Serving-maids,
especially parlour-maids and tweenies, were (and are?) frequently
and unashamedly held by their masters to be a legitimate object of
affection.   Robert Louis Stevenson wrote a poem ("There's just a
twinkle in your eye") with the title *Ne sit ancillæ tibi amor pudori*,
addressed to a "graceful housemaid, tall and fair", but there is no
suggestion he ever followed up his addresses.

The Manx poet T. E. Brown wrote a poem *Ne Sit Ancillae*,
addressed to a "Poor little Teignmouth slavey, Squat, but rosy!
Slatternly, but cosy!"

**Nil volva pulchrius ampla**  *Nothing more beautiful than a sizeable
volva*

Read more about it *s.v. "Pudenda" infra.*

**Noctes ambrosianæ**  *Ambrosian nights, delightful nights*

In the 1820's and 1830's *Blackwood's Magazine* printed a series of
dialogues written by "Christopher North" (John Wilson) under the
title of *Noctes Ambrosianæ*.   These were so named apparently
because they had originated in conversations held in Ambrose's
Tavern, Edinburgh.   However the phrase has been traced back to
the Greek, with Spartan maidens enjoying "nights of ambrosia"
after their exertions of the day.   "Ambrosian nights" certainly now
has sybaritic connotations, with the homeliness of Ambrose's
Tavern being overshadowed by the glamour of "ambrosia".

Ambrosia was the food of the gods on Olympus, conferring
immortality on those who ate it regularly.   Hence "Ambrosian"
carries a hint of carefree nights spent talking, eating and drinking,
with little awareness of the impermanence of youth.

"Altogether it was a very different story from the old festive, unsuspected, club and cricket days, with their *noctes ambrosianæ* at the Albany." E. W. Hornung, *Raffles*.

(There seems to have been some uncertainty about the nature of ambrosia. Some authors said it was a food, others said it was a drink. It was very probably a soup. What the gods drank most regularly was nectar, and consequently, in place of blood, ichor flowed in their veins. It was, incidentally, held to be inadvisable to eat any dead god one might stumble across, since ichor was said to be poisonous to mortals.)

"Other doctors round the county had ditch-water in their veins; he could boast of a pure ichor, to which that of the great Omnium family was but a muddy puddle." Anthony Trollope, *Doctor Thorne*.

## Noli me tangere *Touch me not*

"Jesus saith unto her [*sc.* Mary], Touch me not, for I am not yet ascended to my Father." John xx. 17

Sir Thomas Wyatt wrote a poem, "Whoso list to hunt?", acknowledging sadly that his former mistress, thought to have been Anne Boleyn, had dumped him, now that Henry VIII had begun to take a really close interest in her. The poem concludes with the lines:

"There is written her fair neck round about;
'Noli me tangere; for Caesar's I am,
And wild for to hold, though I seem tame.' "

(According to Solinus, white stags were found 300 years after Julius Caesar's death, their collars inscribed with the command: *Noli me tangere, Caesaris sum*, "Do not touch me, I am Caesar's".)

The wild balsam plant has seed cases which, when ripe and when touched, spring open and scatter their seeds. A common name for the plant is "Touch-me-not" and its scientific name is *Impatiens noli-tangere*.

## Non compos mentis *Not of sound mind, mentally challenged*

*Non compos mentis* is a legal term and since time immemorial has been the centre of learned disputes about what constitutes sanity. It was used by Cicero. Its literal meaning is "not in full possession of one's mental faculties".

The opposite is *compos mentis*, "in full possession of one's faculties". *Compos Mentis* is the name of a Melodic Death/Rock Metal band ("Symphonic Rock from Hell") in Denmark, and also of an Australian Funk band.

"Shakespeare was really a Literary Syndicate. Rainproof [Nogg] is demonstrably *non compos mentis* on that subject, and his infirmity is spreading." Ernest Bramah, "The Ingenious Mind of Mr. Rigby Lacksome."

The phrase *non compos mentis* spawned a noun "non-composser", a useful and exotic (since it does not appear in most modern dictionaries) alternative label for anyone who is intellectually challenged. "If you are not then knocked on the head, your being a non-composser will protect you." J. Fenimore Cooper, *The Last of the Mohicans*.

## Non est inventus  *He cannot be found*

When a writ is served on somebody and that somebody cannot be found, the phrase *Non est* (for *non est inventus*) is (or used to be) written on the writ by the sheriff or bailiff.

"Would that it were not my unhappy duty to inform Your Grace that my journey . . . has met . . . with defeat in the greatest matter. *Non est inventus*." John Fowles, *A Maggot*.

*Non est inventus* is the name of a motet by Manuel Leitão de Aviles.

## Non omnis moriar  *I shall not wholly die*

Horace reckoned that his poetry would outlive him and that he himself, at least in part, would continue to live in his poetry; and he was not mistaken.

"*Non omnis moriar* – if dying I yet live in a tender heart or two." W. M. Thackeray, *Henry Esmond*.

*Non Omnis Moriar* is the motto of the Wimberley family, and is also the name of a track on the album *Domus Mundi* by the Austrian symphonic black metal band Hollenthon.

**Non sequitur** *It does not follow*

A *non sequitur* is a statement which usually causes general bewilderment because it seems somehow not to follow on logically from anything that has been mentioned earlier.

" 'It's all one and the same, for every man who curses the cloth would curse the king if he durst; so for matter o' that, it's all one and the same thing.' 'Excuse me there, Mr. Sergeant,' quoth Partridge, 'that's a *non sequitur*.' 'None of your outlandish linguo (*sic*),' answered the sergeant, leaping from his seat." Henry Fielding, *Tom Jones.*

" 'What a lovely baby!' I said to the young(ish) mother in the supermarket. 'You can 'ave 'im,' she replied. 'I got thirteen more at 'ome.' 'Thirteen!' 'Well, me 'usband snores, don't 'e?' 'Your husband snores, so you've got thir- fourteen children.' My puzzlement at this *non sequitur* must have shown in my face. 'Well, I gotta wear ear-plugs in bed, ain't I? I puts 'em in and 'e comes to bed and says, "Right, are we goin' to go to sleep or what?" And I says, "What?" ' "

**Nunc est bibendum** *Now is (the time) to drink*

Lifted from Horace, this phrase was adopted by the Michelin tyre company as a motto, and Michelin Man himself is also known as "Bibendum". The Bibendum Cafe, Restaurant, Oyster Bar, etc., sits on the forecourt of the Michelin Building in Fulham Road, London, with the motto *Nunc Est Bibendum* freely displayed.

**Nunquam ubi sub ubi** *Never where under where*

A piece of pseudo-Latin which only makes sense when the English is spoken aloud. It heads chapter 45 in Colin Dexter's *The Remorseful Day*, which contains the following passage: "With his own right hand he refastened the top three buttons of the dress he'd specifically requested her to wear above no underwear."

Various reasons have been given for leaving off undergarments. "There was a young lady of Tottenham who'd no manners, or else she'd forgotten 'em. At tea at the vicar's she tore off her knickers, because, she explained, she felt hot in 'em."

**O Dea certe**  *O Goddess beyond doubt!*

Aeneas was the son of Anchises and the goddess of love, who was Aphrodite to the Greeks and Venus to the Romans. Venus seems to done her parenting *in absentia* since when she appeared to Aeneas after his shipwreck near Carthage he failed to recognise her. However he did spot the goddess in her, and addressed her as *Dea certe*.

In Thackeray's *Henry Esmond*, young Henry, on first meeting the Viscountess Castlewood, looked "at her in a sort of delight and wonder, for she had come upon him as a *Dea certe* and appeared the most charming object he had ever looked on".

> "She neither look'd to left nor right,
> Came a tall girl with floating hair,
> Light as a wood-nymph, and as fair.
> *O Dea certe!* – thought poor Dick, . . ."
>> Austin Dobson, *The Noble Patron*.

**Odi profanum vulgus et arceo**  *I hate the common herd and steer clear of them*

Elitism is no modern phenomenon. Horace, as he makes clear here, was not a populariser and wrote only for the cognoscenti of all generations.

Charles Valentin Alkan wrote *c.* 1861 a piece for piano in E flat minor with the title *Odi profanum vulgus et arceo*. It is also the name of a (music) album by Miss Violetta Beauregarde.

*Odi profanum* – "I hate everything profane" – is the motto of the families of Hare and O'Hehir.

**O mihi praeteritos referat si Iuppiter annos**  *If only Jupiter would restore to me the years (that are) fled*

Evander, king of Arcady, is bidding farewell to his son Pallas, who is going with Aeneas to fight the Latins under Turnus. Evander regrets bitterly that age and infirmity prevent him from being one of the party.

In *Goodbye, Mr. Chips*, James Hilton has Chips remark that he had been a master at the school for forty-two years, and had been very happy there. " 'It has been my life,' he said simply. '*O mihi praeteritos referat si Iuppiter annos.*' "

**Omnibus**  *For all*

Our familiar "bus" was not the invention in 1828 of M. Omnibus, a mythical Frenchman, but was designed "for the use of all". The original horse-drawn bus gave way in the twentieth century to the motor-bus, a name that prompted A. D. Godley's poem "What is this that roareth thus? / Can it be a Motor Bus? / Yes, the smell and hideous hum / Indicat Motorem Bum. . . ." (*Vide Appendix II.*)

**Omnium gatherum**  *A comprehensive collection*

*Omnium Gatherum* is the name of an acclaimed black/death metal band from Finland. The phrase is a joke expression, in which *omnium*, "of all", is Latin, while "gather(ing)" has been given a Latin ending in place of the English one.

One of Anthony Trollope's characters in the Barsetshire novels was the Duke of Omnium, and inevitably the name of his ducal seat was Gatherum Castle.

"We . . . looked for a while at Woodgate's bric-à-brac shop, which I never can pass without delaying at the windows – indeed, if I were going to be hanged, I would beg the cart to stop, and let me have one look more at that delightful *omnium gatherum.*" W. M. Thackeray, *Roundabout Papers*.

**Orandum est ut sit mens sana in corpore sano**  *You must pray for a sound mind in a sound body*

"This smiling, bespectacled icon pedals towards us, . . . an advertisement for comradely physical improvement, *mens sana in corpore sano.*" Julian Barnes, *Something to Declare*.

"My predestinated lot in life, alas, has amounted to this: a mens not particularly sana in a corpore not particularly sano". Viscount Mumbles, *A Reflection on My Life*. (Quoted by Colin Dexter in *Daughters of Cain* but Mumbles, being an invention of Dexter himself, is not to be found in Debrett.)

Two cobblers had shops on opposite sides of the village street. One was an educated man, the other was not. One day there appeared in the window of the educated cobbler the sign: "Mens sana in corpore sano". The following day the other cobbler riposted with the sign: "Mens and womens sana in corpore sano".

*Mens Sana in Corpore Sano* is the motto of the Chelsea College of

Physical Education, Eastbourne, and of the Carlton (Australian rules) Football Club.

**Orare est laborare**  To pray is to work

*Vide "Laborare est orare" supra*

**O tempora, o mores**  *O what times!  O what conduct!*

This was Cicero's reaction to the suspicion that Catilina might be planning some sacrilegious crime.  It might be translated loosely as "Fings ain't what they used to be".

Tom Holland, writing in *The Guardian*, used these words in bemoaning the fact that the OCR examination board had decided to abolish the A-level papers in Ancient History.

*O tempora, o mores* is the title of a juvenile poem by Edgar Alan Poe: "O Times!  O Manners!", while Ogden Nash in "The Baffled Hermit" extended the sentiment: "O tempora, O mores, O Montreal!"

**Pabulum**  *Food, fodder*

*Pabulum* is a generic word for food, especially the basic school-meal variety which stuck in our gullets as children and which has stuck in our memories ever since.  Mention need only be made of spam fritters, boiled cabbage, and semolina pudding to bring the memories flooding back.  (Believe it or not, a firm of caterers on the Isle of Wight, supplying tasty and nutritious meals to schools and business enterprises, trade defiantly under the name of "Pabulum".)

The blurb on the 1973 dust cover of *Noblesse Oblige*, edited by Nancy Mitford, states that Miss Mitford's discussion of U-usage "provided conversational pabulum at dinner tables in English-speaking Paris and New York".

Plautus in his *Casina* speaks of *Acherontis pabulum*, "food for Acheron", which is how we all end up: Acheron is a river in Hades.

**Panem et circenses**  *Bread and circuses*

Juvenal suggested that the two things the Roman populace valued above everything were free food and free entertainment.

"The masses are unalterable. . . . Panem et circenses!  Only today

education is one of the bad substitutes for a circus."
D. H. Lawrence, *Lady Chatterley's Lover*.

(In "panem et circenses" both nouns are in the accusative case which is fine if they are the object of the verb. The nominative is "panis et circenses".)

**Panis angelicus**  *Angelic bread, the bread of angels*

The phrase *panis angelicus* occurs in the hymn *Sacris solemniis* (translated as "At this our solemn feast") written by St. Thomas Aquinas for the feast of Corpus Christi. The phrase also introduces verses which were set to music by César Franck as part of his Messe Solonnelle, Op. 12.

Somewhat intriguingly, the phrase "Angel cake" translates into Latin as *Placenta angelica (q.v. infra)*.

**Pari passu**  *With equal pace, together*

"Consider recent history. Industrialism has grown *pari passu* with population." Aldous Huxley, *Eyeless in Gaza*.

". . . Arthur was gone so far away, and his regret and himself were moving towards Arthur, or towards annihilation, *pari passu*, . . ." A. S. Byatt, *Angels and Insects*.

Thomas de Quincey, considering Murder as one of the Fine Arts, calls for an improvement in the style of criticism of masterpieces of murder. "Practice and theory," he says, "must advance *pari passu*."

*Pari Passu Advisory* with its headquarters in Liechtenstein, unites lawyers and partners practising in areas of corporate governance, international banking, finance and tax planning.

**Parturiunt montes nascetur ridiculus mus**  *The mountains labour and shall spawn a laughable little mouse*

Once again this is Horace in *Ars Poetica* ("The Art of Poetry"), now pouring scorn on the labours of his rival poets, who made such a fuss of their efforts but churned out only a load of rubbish.

There has been at least one sighting of this animal in modern literature. W. S. Gilbert, in his poem "Etiquette", ("The *Ballyshannon* foundered off the coast of Cariboo"), has this line: "One day, when out a-hunting for the *mus ridiculus*, . . ."

**Pede claudo** *With halting foot*

The phrase is extracted from one of Horace's *Odes*: *Raro antecedentem scelestum / deseruit pede Poena claudo* – "Rarely has retribution failed to overtake the guilty, though with halting foot and long after the crime." It comes from the same stable as Friedrich von Logau's maxim, translated by Longfellow as: "Though the mills of God grind slowly, yet they grind exceeding small."

"Ay, it must be that: the ghost of some old sin, . . . punishment coming, *pede claudo*, years after memory has forgotten and self-love condoned the fault." R. L. Stevenson, *The Strange Case of Dr. Jekyll and Mr. Hyde*.

"The tramp of the Bobbeian boots may readily be recognised full half a mile away; and *Bill Sykes* has ample time to put his crowbar in his pocket, and vanish round the corner, ere the Peeler, *pede claudo*, can manage to come up to him." *Punch*, 1873.

**Per ardua ad astra** *Through toil to the stars*

*Per ardua ad astra*, the motto of the Royal Flying Corps, formed in 1912, was handed on to the R.F.C.'s successor, the Royal Air Force, on 1st April 1918. It may well be an adaptation of an early Latin tag, *Ad astra per aspera* – "To the stars through difficulties", which itself is the motto of the State of Kansas. To me as an ex-R.A.F. man (A.C.1), the later version sounds an improvement. It might be considered that No. 27 (Bomber) Squadron went one better with their own motto, scorning difficulties: *Quam celerrime ad astra* – "As quickly as possible to the stars".

**Perpetuum mobile** *Perpetual motion*

For centuries inventors have tried to build perpetual motion machines which, once set going, would continue to work *in perpetuum* without the help of any further external impulse. One such inventor was Dr. Algernon Porter of North Carolina (father of the writer O. Henry), who in the latter part of the nineteenth century invented (unsuccessfully), *inter alia*, "a steam-driven automobile, a washing machine, a flying machine, . . . and a water-driven *perpetuum mobile*."

Several composers have written pieces of music whose notes,

played rapidly, all have the same value, and have given them the title of "Perpetuum mobile". These compositions also have the property that all or part of the piece is intended to be repeated, but without a break in the "motion" of the melody when a repeat begins. A well-known *perpetuum mobile* piece, though not labelled as such, is Rimsky-Korsakov's "The Flight of the Bumblebee".

> "...Skrebensky still rocked languidly on the [rocking-] chair....
> 'You look really floppy,' said Gudrun.
> 'I am floppy,' he answered.
> 'Can't you stop?' asked Gudrun.
> 'No – it's the perpetuum mobile.' "
> D. H. Lawrence, *The Rainbow*.

**Per se** *On its own, by itself*

Writing in *The Observer*, Hugh Fearnly-Whittingstall said that Robbins did not object to the flapjack *per se*: "As a snack for someone who is short of energy, it's probably marginally preferable to a Mars Bar."

Philip Larkin in "Round Another Point" suggests that to the person he was addressing, "sex is just sex, an unvarying spasm repeated at intervals, worthless *per se* and meaningless *per se*."

**Persona non grata** *An unacceptable person*

*Persona grata* is a technical phrase used to confirm that a member of a diplomatic mission is acceptable to the country to which he is assigned. If for any reason, or for no reason at all, he is not acceptable, he is then *persona non grata*.

"He [*sc.* Francis] and Celia would have to withdraw to Paris, *persona non grata* in London." Richard Condon, *Any God Will Do*. (It was Francis alone who was *persona non grata* in London, having been declared an undesirable alien following the unfortunate encounter with the belligerent dwarf. In Condon's sentence, it is not made clear which of Francis and Celia was *non grata*. Had both been so, then the phrase would/should have appeared in the plural as *personae non gratae*.)

*Persona non grata* is the name of a book by Jorge Edwards, who was made to feel unwelcome in Cuba; and is also the name of a Polish film by Krzysztof Zanussi.

**Pervigilium Veneris** *The Eve of Venus*

Venus, the goddess of love, was the personification of passion. *Pervigilium Veneris* is an anonymous love poem written *circa* A.D. 350, looking forward eagerly to the feast of Venus, as eagerly as a husband-to-be looks forward to his wedding day (and especially night, even in these relaxed days).

The poem starts with the sentence *Cras amet qui nunquam amavit, Quique amavit cras amet* – "Let him love tomorrow who never loved, whoever loved (before) let him love tomorrow", and these same lines conclude John Fowles' novel, *The Magus*. Evelyn Waugh used *Pervigilium Veneris* for the title of a chapter in *Decline and Fall*, which partly concerns the lamentably fleeting courtship of Paul Pennyfeather and Margot Beste-Chetwynde.

**Placentae angelicae** *Angel cakes*

The *placenta* is well enough known today as the little bag that surrounds us and protects us and helps nourish us when we are in the womb. It is expelled as the afterbirth. The word itself means "(flat) cake" and the name was presumably applied to the afterbirth by Roman physicians who had the sort of warped sense of humour which we and all generations since can appreciate. It is, one could say, the kind of joke that really takes the biscuit.

**Post coitum triste** *After coitus (one is) sad*

Laurence Sterne in *Tristram Shandy* says: ". . . the oily and balsamous parts are of a lively heat and spirit, which accounts for the observation of Aristotle, *'Quod omne animal post coitum est triste'* [Every animal is sad after coitus]". This sentiment finds an echo in Shakespeare's Sonnet 129: "A bliss in proof, and prov'd, a very woe".

The sadness, even though one-sided, more or less, is particularly evident perhaps in those species in which, after copulation, the male is eaten by the female.

In Aldous Huxley's *Point Counter Point*, Philip Quarles suggests that books and lectures are better sorrow-drowners than drink and fornication; "they leave no headache, none of that despairing *post coitum triste* feeling."

"The absence of the object that had unleashed my desire and slaked my thirst made me realise suddenly both the vanity of that desire and the perversity of that thirst. *Omne animal triste post coitum.*"
Umberto Eco, *The Name of the Rose.*

**Post hoc, ergo propter hoc**  *After this, therefore because of this*

This well-known logical fallacy, suggesting that if two things happen at different times, the earlier must be the cause of the later, is quoted by Richard Whately in *Elements of Logic* (1826).

In the recent past there has been a debate about whether or not the MMR vaccine could cause personality disorders in some children. Some experts pointed out that many children showed symptoms of such disorders after they had been vaccinated. Defenders of the vaccine claimed that there was no firm evidence that it was harmful, and suggested that those who claimed otherwise were arguing fallaciously along *post hoc, ergo propter hoc* lines.

**Post mortem**  *After death*

Nowadays a "post mortem" may well involve slicing up a body to determine the cause of death. In the Middle Ages, however, an *inquisitio post mortem* held after the death of a prominent man or woman was a less bloody affair, being a routine judicial enquiry into how much property the deceased owned, what services he or she owed to an overlord or to the Crown, and especially and urgently who might be the rightful heirs to the deceased's property.

From *inquisitio* we obtain our word "inquest". An amazing number of documents recording the results of such enquiries over many centuries is held in the National Records Office, and photocopies may be had on request.

Post-mortem photography (also known as memorial portraiture, *memento mori* or mourning portraits) was the practice of photographing the recently deceased. This was especially common with infants and young children, since Victorian era childhood mortality rates were extremely high, and a post-mortem photograph might have been the only image of the child the family ever had.

**Praemonitus, praemunitus** *Forewarned is forearmed*

*Praemonitus, praemunitus* is the motto of the Intelligence School of the RAF.

The Whittemore-Durgin Glass Co. of Rockland, Maine, offer free gifts with their products but advise that if anyone tries ordering just free stuff alone, "you'll still have to pay minimum shipping charges. *Praemonitus, praemunitus*".

**Proxime accessit** *Came (close) second*

*Proxime accessit* is a term which may appear on the lists of prizewinners in the ancient universities to indicate those who didn't quite come first. Some of the more tender-hearted institutions however award a "Proxime Accessit" prize as a consolation. Carmel College in Aukland, New Zealand, awards both a "Dux" ("Leader") Cup and a "Proxime Accessit ad Ducem" ("second to the Dux") Cup each year.

**Pudenda** *Things to be ashamed of*

*Pudenda* are in particular those body parts which, when on a nudist beach, we may display more or less proudly according to the degree of our natural endowments, but which we tend to keep modestly covered up in Waitrose or in Westminster Abbey, unless we happen to be very young and very feminine.

The *pudenda* include A. P. Herbert's "portions of a woman that appeal to man's depravity"; which "are constructed with considerable care"; and to which doctors have given "delightful Latin names". Many of these delightful names started off life as euphemisms. The *vagina*, for instance, is technically (and botanically) a sheath: every good blade should possess one.

The *vulva* is literally "a wrapping" and could be applied to such things as the white of an egg, which was wrapped round the yolk. The preferred spelling in Latin seems to have been *volva*, which partly at least excuses my wife's query when a girl friend acquired a new Volvo Estate: "Has Peter tried out your new Vulva?" To the Romans, *vulva* or *volva* also meant "womb", but an animal womb rather than a human one. According to Horace, who came of humble farming stock and so should know, a great delicacy on the Roman farmer's table (*mensa*) was sow's womb – *nil volva pulchrius ampla* or "nothing more beautiful than a sizeable *volva*". (Note: The Romans were inclined to mix the order of their words in a manner we often find somewhat confusing. So: *nil pulchrius ampla volva* = nothing / more beautiful / than a sizeable / volva.)

Bits associated with the vulva are the greater and lesser "lips", the *labia majora* and the *labia minora*. For more details of these see any good children's book on "Where do we come from?"

Two more of A.P.H.'s "delightful Latin names" are *hymen* and *clitoris*, but these are Greek, not Latin, and so count as euphemisms because the best way of avoiding using the rude vernacular term for a *pudendum* (singular of *pudenda*) is to borrow the relevant word from some foreign tongue, as in "pardon my French".

In Greek *hymen* was a membrane, and a Greek bat could be described as *hymenopteros*, "membrane-winged". For biologists *Hymenoptera* is an order of insects, including the bees and wasps, which have four transparent wings. *Clitoris* was apparently *kleitoris* in Greek, but my Greek dictionary doesn't seem to have an entry under this heading, perhaps, since it is a family dictionary, with good reason.

Men also possess pudenda. In *The Name of the Rose* Umberto Eco notes that the features of the dead man were swollen. "The body . . . seemed a woman's except for the obscene spectacle of the flaccid *pudenda*."

Perhaps not surprisingly the male pudenda boast few if any particularly delightful names, Latin or otherwise. The word *penis* was itself a Latin euphemism, its original meaning being simply "a tail". However we have a further Latin euphemism for this original euphemism, viz, *membrum virile*, the "male member". (*Virile* is pronounced as three syllables, vi-ri-le, just as is "recipe".)

"[Doctor Swain]'s considered quite a competent quack, they tell me."

"To be honest, I thought he was a bit of a . . ."

"Bit of a *membrum virile*? . . ."

Here Colin Dexter, in *The Jewel that was Ours*, overhears Morse chatting with Max, the pathologist. It is clear that Morse, as I do, hesitates through a certain delicacy to use the word "pr-ck".

**Quam celerrime** *As quickly as possible*

A horse called *Quam Celerrime* may well be running today at Haydock Park.

" 'Get the same car, Kershaw – nice, comfy seats – and pick me up from home *quam celerrime*.' 'Pardon?' 'Smartish!' " Colin Dexter, The *Remorseful Day*.

The full Latin phrase would be *quam celerrime potest* – "as quickly as can be".

**Quid pro quo** *Something equivalent in return*

F. P. Smoler, writing in *The Observer*, mentions "the gangster Frank Costello, with whom [J. Edgar] Hoover had a notorious *quid pro quo*", a mutual understanding of give and take.

When the secretary of a village football club wrote asking a town club of somewhat higher standing for a friendly match, the secretary of the other club wrote suggesting a date for the game "providing you will be willing to give us a *quid pro quo*", i.e., a return game. The first secretary replied saying: "My committee has asked me to send the pound for the professional you mentioned, although they are surprised at such a request from a club of your standing".

The technically correct plural of *quid pro quo* is either *qua pro quo* or *quæ pro quo*, but it seems sensible to follow the example of such writers as Ivor Brown who, in *Chosen Words*, mentioned *quids pro quo*. This is certainly preferable to *quid pro quos*.

**Quota** *A share*

A term based on the Latin *quot?* – "how many?" and familiar from its use in determining how much fish, milk, etc, a particular person or organization may catch, produce, market, import or export.

"Richard was careful to put in his daily quota of press-ups – twenty before breakfast, twenty after lunch, and twenty coming home on the train." P. J. Dorricot, *Tales out of the Nursery*.

**Quo vadis?** *Whither goest thou?*

Jesus tells his disciples (John xvi. 5): "But now I go my way to him that sent me; and none of you asketh me, Whither goest thou?"

At a later date, so the legend has it, St. Peter was fleeing from certain death in Rome when he met Jesus, and asked Him this question. Jesus replied that He was going to Rome to be crucified again. Suitably shamed, Peter returned to Rome to meet his own fate.

As well as being the name of a restaurant in London, *Quo Vadis* was the name of a book written by Henryk Sienkiewicz in 1896, and subsequently made into a film in 1902. Other films followed, the best-known being made in 1951 and starring Robert Taylor and Deborah Kerr.

*Quo vadis sequimur* – "Whither thou goest we follow" – is the motto of Didsbury College, Bristol.

## Rara avis (in terris, nigroque simillima cycno) *A rare bird (on earth, like a black swan)*

According to Juvenal, a *rara avis* was a chaste and faithful wife. Since neither he nor his readers knew anything of the black swans of Australia, his simile carried weight enough . He also said, no doubt prudently and as an afterthought, that a good man is a rare animal too: *Vir bonum est animal rarum.*

*Rara Avis* is the name of an Alternative band from Bratislava and also of a rain-forest reserve in Costa Rica.

Writing in *The Independent* about Lorenzo the Magnificent, Jeremy Sams said that "he was after all, that *rara avis*, a Jewish Catholic priest with a wife and children".

## Requiescat in pace (R.I.P.) *May he/she rest in peace*

R.I.P. is a common inscription on tombstones and memorial tablets.

"Lady Mary did not live long after her return to England. . . . *Requiescat in pace*; for she quarrelled all her life." W. Bagehot, *Literary Essays*, "Lady Mary Wortley Montague".

"After running up the house [the mine-owner] finds he only had $2.80 left to furnish it with, so he invests that in whisky and jumps off the roof on a spot where he now requiescats in pieces." O. Henry, "The Chair of Philanthromathematics".

In *The Oxford Book of English Verse*, the heading *Requiescat* is given to Matthew Arnold's poem, "Strew on her roses, roses, And never a spray of yew. In quiet she reposes: . . ."

**Resurgam**  *I shall rise again*

This brief gravestone inscription was popular in the sixteenth and seventeenth centuries, but seems later to have dropped out of favour.

"[Helen's] grave is in Brocklebridge Churchyard: for fifteen years after her death it was only covered by a grassy mound; but now a gray marble tablet marks the spot, inscribed with her name, and the word '*Resurgam*'." Charlotte Brontë, *Jane Eyre*.

"Resurgam" was the name given to the first mechanically-powered (steam-driven) British submarine, designed and built by Rev. George Garrett in 1879. The name clearly reflected her builder's confidence in her buoyancy and in her ability to resurface, and her trials did indeed prove successful, although unfortunately she was lost at sea when under tow in 1880.

A lump of stone excavated from the ruins of Old St. Paul's, destroyed in the Great Fire of London, 1666, is said to have borne the inscription *Resurgam*, offering promise of the successful rebuilding of the cathedral. "Resurgam" is the motto of the families of Blake of Tillmouth and of Stewart of New Hall, and of the city of Portland, Maine, the motto here referring to Portland's recoveries from four devastating fires.

**Rigor mortis**  *A stiffening of the body in death*

A stiffening, it seems, not only in death, but occasionally in life also. In Richard Gordon's *Doctor in the House*, "Rigor Mortis" was the nickname given to a particularly unbending nurse.

*Rigor Mortis* is the name of a Thrash Metal band founded in Texas.

Writing in *The Guardian* Ian Buruma suggested that making a utensil as a pure work of art "can lead to decadence, when the stylised performance hardens into a kind of aesthetic *rigor mortis.*"

**Rigor vitae**  *A stiffening of the body in life*

**Sic volo, sic jubeo**  *Such is my will, such is my command*

In his *Satires*, vi. 223, Juvenal presents the picture of a vindictive wife demanding of a hen-pecked husband that a slave be crucified for an imaginary misdemeanour. When asked (hesitatingly) why, she replied: *Hoc volo, sic iubeo, sit pro ratione voluntas* – "This I wish, thus I command, let my will be reason (enough)." From this derives the (fairly) more commonly used phrase, *sic volo, sic iubeo*.

"When Lady Kew said *Sic volo, sic jubeo*, I promise you few persons of her ladyship's belongings stopped, before they did her biddings, to ask her reasons." W. M. Thackeray, *The Newcomes*.

A review of Georges Duby's *France in the Middle Ages* recognises that "It is a major tribute . . . that he has been able to deal with publishers in his *sic volo sic iubeo* style."

"Surely you're not mowing the lawn at this time of the year? It's mid-winter!" "I'm doing it to please my wife. She wanted it done." "Why?" "*Sic volo, sic iubeo*. Who can fathom the workings of a woman's mind?"

**Simplex munditiis** *Simple in (your/her/his/their) elegance*

In this complimentary manner Horace addresses his *quondam* girlfriend: "Pyrrha, . . . simple in thy elegance".

In *The Oxford Book of English Verse*, the heading *Simplex Munditiis* is given to Ben Jonson's poem, "Still to be neat, still to be drest / As you were going to a feast; . . ." reprimanding a girl who was always and unfailingly dressed up to the nines. *Simplex Munditiis* is the motto of Viscount Simonds, and of the families of Philips and of Symonds of Pilsdon.

"I should be glad to see you the instrument of introducing into our style that simplicity which is the best and truest ornament of most things in life, which the politer age always aimed at in their building and dress, *simplex munditiis*, as well as in their productions of wit." Jonathan Swift, "On Style".

**Sine nomine** *Without a name*

This is a sort of default name for anything for which one cannot think up a suitable alternative and distinctive name. It is the name of the tune by Ralph Vaughan Williams to which is usually sung the hymn "For all the saints", and which is no doubt in the repertoire of the Sine Nomine International Touring Choir.

*Sine Nomine Publishing* is a marque dedicated to the finest in sandbox role-playing games and supplements.

**Sine qua non**  *Without which nothing*

During much of his working life in London (which lasted for close on eighty years until he was ninety-four) my father invariably carried a rolled black umbrella, a *sine qua non* for the well-dressed businessman-about-town.

"It is a *sine qua non* of the Coarse costume that it is impossible to move in it." Michael Green, *The Art of Coarse Acting*.

In Nichola Thorne's *Never Such Innocence*, Constance had been taught that "respect for her elders was a *sine qua non* of existence".

Speaking on the radio about grassland, a government farming expert once famously remarked that a *sine qua non* of a good ley was a firm bottom.

**Siste, viator**  *Pause, traveller*

An invitation, dating from Roman times, to passers-by to pause long enough to read an inscription on a tomb or memorial.

*Siste Viator* is the name of a book of poems by Sarah Manguso.

**Si vis pacem, para bellum**  *If you want peace, prepare for war*

This is the gist of a helpful suggestion urged by Vegetius *c.* 390 B.C. in his *De Rei Militari* – "On War". It is the motto of 604 Squadron (County of Middlesex) of the Auxiliary Air Force.

In its peace-keeping role NATO adopted the 9 mm Luger Parabellum cartridge for use in pistols and sub-machine-guns.

**Solvitur ambulando**  *It is solved by walking*

Solved, that is, by peering into odd corners and by poking one's nose into other people's business, rather than by just sitting and cogitating on the details of the crime supplied by someone else. Colin Dexter heads chapter 13 of *The Jewel that was Ours* with this phrase. It is also for some reason the motto of the family of Lord Pearson.

In "What the Tortoise said to Achilles", Lewis Carroll looks at Zeno's paradox in which Achilles is chasing a tortoise. Achilles starts at point A, the tortoise at point B. When Achilles arrives at B, the tortoise has moved on to point C. When Achilles arrives at C, the tortoise has moved on to D, and so *ad infinitum*. By this argument Achilles can never catch up with the tortoise. However, in a trial run set up by Carroll, Achilles does not even have to break into a trot to overtake the tortoise. " 'It can be done,' said Achilles. 'It has been done! *Solvitur ambulando.*' "

By his own admission, the travel writer Patrick Leigh Fermor was a "rather rackety" figure before he struggled back to health through walking. He became, relatively late in life, a mentor to the younger writer Bruce Chatwin, who adopted Leigh Fermor's motto, *Solvitur Ambulando* – "It is solved by walking".

### Splendide mendax  *Splendidly false, or Nobly untruthful*

Horace was in love with Lyde, a timid girl. Hoping to persuade her to throw caution to the winds, he placed before her past examples of feminine daring. Here he is heaping praise on Hypermnestra, one of the fifty daughters of Danaus. Danaus had been more or less forced to agree to the marriage of his daughters to their fifty cousins, but in revenge had determined to convert fifty wives into fifty widows by the simple expedient of having each of his daughters cut off her husband's head on their wedding night. Hypermnestra alone drew back from performing this grisly duty, breaking her promise to her father and warning her husband to fly for his life, having presumably first satisfied herself that he was worth saving. The phrase *splendide mendax* has appealed to writers ever since, and it is used particularly to applaud the use of feminine wiles when these are employed for humanitarian ends.

The charge was levelled not only at women. The frontispiece to an early edition of *Gulliver's Travels* shows Gulliver's picture with below it the comment "*Splendide mendax*", a hint perhaps that Gulliver's tales were to be taken *cum grano salis*.

*Splendide mendax* is the name of a music track by John Badger and the Moustache Riders of Doom.

"Splendide mendax" is the *locus classicus* of an oxymoron.

### Status quo (ante)  *Previous state, situation*

"The exact mind which of all others dislikes the stupid adherence to the *status quo*, is the keen, quiet, improving Whig mind; . . ." W. Bagehot, "The First Edinburgh Reviewers."

> "Nature, and Nature's laws, lay hid in night,
> God said, *Let Newton be!* and all was light." Alexander Pope.

"It did not last: the Devil howling *Ho,*
*Let Einstein be*, restored the status quo." Sir John Squire.

"Status Quo" for no apparent reason is the name of a well-known popular music group.

**Stella maris** *Star of the sea*

Early Christian sailors, prompted possibly by St. Jerome, adopted the Blessed Virgin Mary as their patron saint and protector and bestowed this title on her. *Stella Maris* was the name of a 1918 film starring Mary Pickford, and is also the motto of Broadstairs Urban District Council in Kent.

**Stet** *Let it stand*

*Stet* is a mark used by a printer's reader when he has second thoughts about a section of copy, reversing his original decision to change or delete it.

Diana Athill wrote a book about her life as a publisher and called it *Stet*.

**Sui generis** *Of its own kind, "one of a kind"*

Writing in *The Observer,* Anthony Burgess said of Angus Wilson's *The Old Men at the Zoo* that "the genre was unclear . . . but is now perhaps seen as *sui generis*; . . ." Mr. Burgess here neatly mixes three languages, the import of his judgement being that the genre is a genre of its own, and can be subsumed into no other *genus*.

"Jacqueline was a very remarkable person, a rare spirit, a woman *sui generis*." Q. Q. Enwright, *Mistress and Maid*.

Sometimes used in the sense of "one-off". "Peppone wrinkled his forehead. 'Monsignore,' he explained solemnly, 'it was a question of a *casus belli*, an affair *sui generis*, as they say.' " Giovanni Guareschi, *The Little World of Don Camillo*.

**Sunt lacrimae rerum et mentem mortalia tangunt** *Tears abound in all things and human suffering touches the heart*

According to Virgil this was Aeneas' cry of grief when he saw scenes of the battle of Troy depicted in carvings on the walls of the temple in Carthage. His tears were forced from him particularly by the image of King Priam.

"Mackail, who had married Burne-Jones' daughter, gave to his Virgil an eightyish air, the *lacrimae rerum* spilled over . . . with a morbid distress." Cyril Connolly, *Enemies of Promise*.

Robert Frobisher's suicide note in David Mitchell's *Cloud Atlas* concludes with the words *Sunt lacrimæ rerum*; while the whole seven-word quotation furnishes a heading to chapter 34 in Colin Dexter's *The Remorseful Day*.

Carl Orff wrote an *a capella* piece for six male voices called *Sunt lacrimæ rerum*.

### Supera moras  *Overcome delays*

*Supera moras* is the motto of Bolton Wanderers Football Club. It also translates roughly as "Get your finger out".

### Suum cuique bene olet  *What is one's own smells sweet*

Erasmus, in his *Adagia,* left his readers to supply for themselves the answer to "one's own what?" The implication is that whatever it is doesn't necessarily smell that sweet to others.

"Does not Freud underrate the extent to which nothing, in private, is really shocking as long as it belongs to ourselves? *Suum cuique bene olet*." C. S. Lewis, "Psycho-analysis and Literary Criticism".

*Suum Cuique* is the title of a poem by Ralph Waldo Emerson, "The rain has spoiled the farmer's day . . . I will attend my proper cares."

### Tabula rasa  *A clean slate*

The human brain at birth, and before it becomes cluttered with a load of useless information, is often referred to as a *tabula rasa*. Peter Conrad in a book review in *The Observer* says: "Locke remarked, thinking of the *tabula rasa* of the infantile mind, that in the beginning all the world was America."

"I want to lay my life before her, don't you see? I'm starting over, I'm clean, I'm *tabula rasa*, . . ." Julian Barnes, *Talking It Over*.

It might have been better if the journalist who talked about theories that "children are not 'tabula rasa' ", had opted to use the plural form, which is *tabulae rasae*.

The motto of the Laurel and Hardy fan club, "The Sons of the Desert", is *Duae tabulae rasae in quibus nihil scriptum est* – "two clean slates on which nothing has been written" or "two minds without a single thought."

**Taedium vitae** *Boredom, the tedium of living*

*Taedium Vitae* is the second demo (instrumental) by the Russian power metal band Catharsis, and is also the name of a rock/gothic/post punk band from Nantes.

This phrase together with *timor mortis conturbat me (q.v infra)* translates directly into Joe's sentiment in the song "Ol' Man River" from Jerome Kern's *Show Boat* – "Ah'm tired of livin' an' skeered of dyin'."

"The notion of liberty amuses the people of England, and helps to keep off the *tædium vitæ*." James Boswell, *The Life of Samuel Johnson, LL.D.*

Oscar Wilde wrote a poem with the title *Tædium Vitæ* – "To stab my youth with desperate knives . . ." In *The Picture of Dorian Gray*, Wilde decribes the hero of a novel as being "sick with that *ennui*, that terrible *tædium vitæ*, that comes on those to whom life denies nothing."

**Tandem** *At length*

Here we have a rare classical pun. As Grose's *Dictionary of the Vulgar Tongue* (1785) has it: "Tandem – a two-wheeled chaise, buggy or noddy, drawn by two horses, one before the other, that is *at length*." A randem-tandem had three horses instead of two, but still in line one behind the other. The tandem bicycle appeared on the roads *circa* 1884.

Sometimes the phrase "in tandem" is used (confusingly) to mean "together with" or even "side by side". There was indeed a "sociable tricycle" made in the early 1880's on which the riders sat side by side, but a proper tandem has them "one after the other".

The "Tandem Heart" is a "percutaneously inserted ventricular assist device that can be used as temporary resuscitation after an acute myocardial infarction or a long term bridge to heart transplant for patients with severe cardiomyopathy."

**Tempus edax rerum** *Time the devourer of things*

*Tempus edax rerum* is the name of a Doom Black Metal group in Brazil.

" 'Mr. Western a daughter grown up!' cries the barber. 'I remember the father a boy; well, *tempus edax rerum*!' " Henry Fielding, *Tom Jones*.

But we must be fair, for Time is also a healer, and the same speaker acknowledged this later. " 'Time, however, the best physician of the mind, at length brought me relief.' 'Ay, ay; *tempus edax rerum*,' said Partridge."

*Tempus edax rerum* appears on a old sundial which was fixed over the south doorway of Gulval Church, near Penzance, until thieves stole it in 1998. It is tempting, albeit unchristian, to hope something nasty devours them, even if it is only remorse.

**Tempus fugit** *Time flies (or flees)*

This distils the essence from Virgil's *Sed fugit interea, fugit inreparabile tempus* – "Time is fleeing, fleeing beyond recall."

"Yet, in asking that question [about the future of GMTV], there is also an inevitable feeling of *tempus fugit*." Report in *The Guardian*.

I was told the following story by an elderly and rather prim lady I met in Eastbourne many years ago.

Two old folk were sitting on a sea-front bench contemplating the evening scene. One said, "Well, *tempus fugit* be creeping on." The other replied, "Yes, they be creeping on me too."

**Terra incognita** *The Unknown Land*

About the only *terra incognita* left in the world now, apart from a small area of Norfolk, is Antarctica, the last of the unexplored regions of the earth. The phrase is still in popular use however and Google presents 1,260,000 choices to the searcher.

David Mitchell, in *Cloud Atlas*, says that all his life, sophisticated, idiotic women have taken it upon themselves "to *understand* me, to *cure* me, but Eva knows I'm *terra incognita*, and explores me unhurriedly, like you did".

"So there I am in some *terra incognita* by the name of Stoke

Newington . . ." Julian Barnes, *Talking It Over*.

In its plural form and in a non-geographical sense, S. T. Coleridge used the term in his notes on Shakespeare's *Richard II*. ". . . mark in this scene (ii.2) Shakespeare's gentleness in touching the tender superstitions, the *terræ incognitæ* of presentiments, in the human mind; . . ."

## Tertium quid  *A third something*

In alchemy, a mixture of two things which differs noticeably from both.

In "The Chemist to his Love", (author unknown), the chemist laments that if only his love could be potassium and he *aqua fortis*, they would together become nitrate of potash, and live happily "until death should decompose the fleshly *tertium quid*."

*Tertium quid* was used in the Christological debates of the fourth century with reference to the followers of Apollinaris who spoke of Christ as something neither human nor divine, but a mixture of the two, and therefore a "third thing".

More recently *tertium quid* has been used to refer to the uncertain or missing element in a trio of things or persons, when two of the trio are already known. In Erskine Childers' *The Riddle of the Sands,* the narrator so refers to an unknown member of the opposing camp: "Her skipper's safe anyway; so's Böhme, so's the Tertium Quid, . . ." Rudyard Kipling in *Wee Willie Winkie*; "At the Pit's Mouth", states: "Once upon a time there was a Man and his Wife and a Tertium Quid." Robert Browning gave the title *Tertium Quid* to his fourth book of "The Ring and the Book". Had Carol Reed's film "The Third Man" been made in Ancient Rome, it might conceivably have been entitled *Tertium Quid*.

## Timor mortis conturbat me  *The fear of death disturbs me*

This refrain from the Roman Catholic Office of the Dead encourages us to admit our secret fears. It is used by William Dunbar in his poem "Lament for the Makaris" (makers, *sc.* poets). In the poem he rehearses the names of twenty-four poets who have died recently and of another who is *in extremis*: surely Dunbar himself must be next in line.

I that in heill was and gladness
Am trublit now with great sickness
And feblit with infirmitie: –
*Timor mortis conturbat me.*

" 'I don't want to die, why should I? . . . But . . . it doesn't interest me, you know.'
"  ' "Timor mortis conturbat me",' quoted Birkin. "
D. H. Lawrence, *Women in Love.*

**Tityre, tu patulae recubans sub tegmine fagi** *Tityrus, thou lying canopied beneath thy spreading beech-tree*

Tityrus was clearly an idle upper-class layabout, and the name "Tityre-tu" attached itself in the 17th century to a group of aristocratic hooligans who, having become bored with lying canopied, etc., had nothing better to do with their energy than run riot and cause trouble in the streets.

Longfellow translated the whole poem: "Tityrus, thou in the shade of a spreading beech-tree reclining, . . ."

"Nosey senior . . . was reposing *sub tegmine fagi* . . . , in a sort of tea-garden arbour, overlooking a dung-heap." R. S. Surtees, *Jorrocks' Jaunts and Jollities.*

*Sub Tegmine Fagi* is the inescapable motto of the family of Beech of Brandon Hall, Coventry.

**Totis viribus** *With all (my) strength*

"I have passed over all the Doctor's other reproaches upon Scotland but the sheep's head I will defend *totis viribus*." James Boswell, *The Life of Samuel Johnson, LL.D.*

*Totis Viribus* was the motto of Goode, Durrant & Murray (Consolidated) Ltd., an Australian firm which dealt in Wheatstone Anglo concertinas until it was taken over by another firm in 1985. *Totis Viribus* is also the motto of 414 (Black Knight) Squadron of the Royal Canadian Air Force, and of Epsom Normal Primary School, New Zealand.

**Trivia** *Trifles*

*Trivia* are perhaps best defined as being trivial.

In the recent past a regular column entitled "Film Trivia" appeared the *Radio Times*, relating unimportant though not uninteresting stories connected with the making of well-known films.

## Ultima Thule *Farthest Thule*

Virgil in his *Georgics* mentions *Ultima Thule*, the island which is the northernmost part of Earth's dry land. Longfellow wrote a clutch of poems under the general title *Ultima Thule*, of which one contains the line "Ultima Thule! Utmost Isle!"

In "The Pit and the Pendulum", Edgar Allan Poe uses the phrase in a non-geographical sense. ". . . *the pit*, typical of hell and regarded by rumour as the Ultima Thule of all [the Inquisition's] punishments."

Thule works in both directions, north and south. "Thule" is the name given to one of the northernmost settlements in Greenland, while a small rock in the South Atlantic is called "South Thule".

## Ultra vires *Beyond one's powers*

Most organizations, committees and courts of law have a constitution, written or otherwise, which defines their duties and states in explicit terms what power they have to see that their decisions are acted on. If they craftily try to do anything which is beyond this agreed but restricted power, they are acting *ultra vires* and can be called to account by a higher authority for their excess enthusiasm.

## Vade mecum *Go with me*

Second-hand bookshops are full of old phrase-books with such titles as *The Traveller's Vade Mecum in Germany*. Anthony Burgess once confided in *The Observer* that "when I was an undergraduate, this tome [T. S. Eliot's *Selected Essays*] . . . was a *vade mecum*." *Vade Mecum* is the name of a Plucker document viewer for the pocket PC.

In "The Girl and the Habit", O. Henry laments the withdrawal from the fraternity of writers of all sources of inspiration other than that of "the reliable, old, unassailable vade mecum – the unabridged dictionary".

The phrase might also be loosely translated as "come with me". There can be little doubt that Ernest Bramah had *vade mecum* in mind when he referred in *The Moon of Much Gladness* to "The Official Executioner's Come-with-Me and Complete Torturer's Fireside Companion".

**Veni, vidi, vici** *I came, I saw, I conquered*

Julius Caesar sent this early version of a text message to Amantius in 47 B.C., announcing his victory over Pharnaces at Zela in Pontus.

Tawdry Hepburn, the San Francisco indie-rock loungecore group, uses "Veni vidi vici" as a refrain in "Sink", a song about mythic female dominance borrowed from the rock group Apocalipstick.

In October 2005 *The Guardian*, advertising a T.V. series on ancient Rome, used an inscription which read: "*Veni, vidi, volo domum redire*" – "I came, I saw, I want to go home".

*Vidi Vici* is the motto of 191 Squadron of the R.A.F., whilst *Veni, vidi, Visa* ("We came, we saw, we went shopping") is the motto of Sally Poplin.

**Via Dolorosa** *The Way of Sorrows*

The *Via Dolorosa* led Christ from "Olivet to Calvary", from his arrest on the Mount of Olives, also called Gethsemane, to his crucifixion on the hill called Calvary (or Golgotha). The "Stations of the Cross" mark stages on this journey, beginning at the judgment chamber and finishing in the tomb in which Christ's body was laid. When the "Stations" are performed in public, it is customary to sing stanzas from the hymn "Stabat Mater" whilst walking from one Station to the next.

"Now the traveller [in Ypres] along that Via Dolorosa, the Menin Road, begins scrunching into smaller fragments with his boots, bits of the glorious old stained glass of the Cathedral lying broken among its stones." Report in *The Guardian*, March 1919.

In *Mapp and Lucia*, E. E. Benson portrays Major Benjy as making "the passage of his Via Dolorosa to glean the objects he had dropped" when retrieving his belongings, which included his false teeth, thrown out from Elisabeth Mapp's house.

*Via Dolorosa* is the name of a Eutropia Universe society, and also the name of a monologue about the Middle East written and performed by David Hare.

**Video meliora proboque; deteriora sequor** *I see and approve the better (path), but follow the worse*

Ovid reports that Jason, leader of the Argonauts, had asked Æetes, king of Colchis, to surrender the Golden Fleece. Æetes said he would do this only after Jason had completed three near-impossible tasks, involving coping with such capricious beings as dragons and fire-breathing bulls. Fortunately Æetes' daughter, Medea, through the agency of Hero, Aphrodite and Eros, had fallen helplessly in love with Jason and was determined to help him (the "*deteriora*") using her magic powers, in opposition to her father's wishes (the "*meliora*"). With her help Jason succeeded in all the three tasks aforementioned and left Colchis taking with him both the fleece and, possibly wrapped in it, Medea.

In Aldous Huxley's *Eyeless in Gaza*, Antony B. notes in his diary that "Five words sum up every biography. *Video meliora proboque; deteriora sequor.*" Like all other human beings, he knew what he ought to do, but continued to do what he knew he ought not to do.

". . . he taught me to see and approve better things. 'Tis my own fault, *deteriora sequi*." W. M. Thackeray, *Henry Esmond*. ("Sequi" is "to follow".)

*Meliora sequamur* – "May we follow the better path", is the aspiring motto of both Brighton Boys' Grammar School and Blackpool Boys' Grammar School, and also of the Borough of Eastbourne.

**Virginibus puerisque (canto)** *To maidens and young men (I sing)*

Horace is here defining his target audience, after having disclaimed any interest in the common herd, the *profanum vulgus* of *Odi profanum vulgus* (*q.v. supra*).

Taking on himself the mantle of an Agony Aunt, Robert Louis Stephenson wrote a book addressed to maidens and young men with the title *Virginibus Puerisque*, which included *inter alia* a number of essays on the problems of young adulthood and their tentative solutions.

*Virginibus puerisque* is also the title of a poem by Alan Seeger, killed in action in France in 1916 while serving with the French Foreign Legion. He was uncle of the folk singer Pete Seeger.

Julian Barnes in *Talking It Over* says he had only to dangle his aromatically forged reference from the Hamlet Academy before Mr. Tim and "there I was, unleashed before the cosmopolitan *virginibus puerisque* couchant before their desks."

**Virgo intacta** *A virgin*

"The Virgo Intacta" are a Jazz-Punk band originally from Leigh-on-Sea, Essex.

Catullus uses the phrase *virgo intacta* in one of his many *Odes*. Presumably the opposite is *virgo tacta*, "a maiden touched" but on this point Catullus is not forthcoming. It appears that many Roman girls were given in marriage when they were no more than twelve years old, the Roman *paterfamilias* thereby neatly solving the problem of the wayward teenage daughter creating havoc in his household. It also appears that to the Romans *virgo* was any young girl, married or unmarried, intact or otherwise.

**Vis inertiae** *The power of inertia, of inactivity*

Newton defines *vis inertiæ* as a power inherent in all matter, by which it resists any attempt to change its state, either of rest or motion. (Many of us know the feeling.)

"I have thought of a pulley to raise me gradually [out of bed]; but that would give me pain, as it would counteract my internal inclination. I would have something that can dissipate the *vis inertiæ*, and give elasticity to the muscles." James Boswell. *The Life of Samuel Johnson, LL.D.*

**Vis medicatrix naturae** *The healing power of Nature*

*Vis Medicatrix Naturae* is the name of a firm established in Portland, Oregon, by two naturopathic physicians, supplying natural medicines.

In Aldous Huxley's *After Many a Summer*, the Fifth Earl of Gonister is not sure whether he owes his recovery "to the Carp, to the Return of Spring, or to the *Vis medicatrix Naturae*."

" 'I am a great believer in nature's remedies, *vis medicatrix naturae*,' explained Uncle Walter, sneezing a little as he mixed himself a hot whisky and lemon." P. J. Dorricot, *Beyond the Nursery Slopes*.

111

**Vixi puellis nuper idoneus**  *In those days I lived equipped for ladies' love*

Horace is resigning himself to the fact that with advancing years the amorous capabilities of his wedding apparatus are sadly declining.

In Patrick O'Brian's *The Surgeon's Mate,* Sir Joseph Blaine admits to having become most painfully aware of "a certain want of vigour . . . as though I too should sing *vixi puellis nuper idoneus . . .*"

**Vox et praeterea nihil**  *A voice and nothing more*

*Vox et praeterea nihil* is the name of an album by the Ambient group "Controlled Dissonance".

Ovid has been credited with being the first to say this but the phrase doesn't seem to appear anywhere in his works, although in his *Metamorphoses* he tells the apposite story of the two lovers, Echo and Narcissus. Narcissus fell in love with his own reflection in water and grew increasingly inattentive to Echo's charms, so that in despair she gradually faded away and finally became a disembodied voice. It was probably left to Plutarch in his *Laconic Apophthegms* to put the words *Vox et praeterea nihil* into the mouth of the Lacedemonian hunter, dismayed when a nightingale, which he had lovingly plucked, drawn and quartered ready for the pot, proves to be "all voice and nothing else".

The phrase can also be used in the sense of "all talk and no action". Patrick O'Brian, in *The Mauritius Command*, dismisses a shipman as ". . . a poor groatsworth of a man, *vox et praeterea nihil* (though a very fine *vox*) . . .".

## Appendix I

### From *The Bankolidaid*, Lib.1 By F. Sidgwick

Charmer virumque I sing, Jack plumigeramque Arabellam.
Costermonger erat Jack Jones, asinumque agitabat;
In Covent Garden holus, sprouts vendidit asparagumque.
Vendidit in Circo to the toffs Arabella the donah,
Qua Piccadilly propinquat to Shaftesbury Avenue, flores.

Jam Whitmonday adest; ex Newington Causeway the costers
Erumpunt multi celebrare their annual beano;
Quisque suum billycock habuere et donah ferentes,
Impositique rotis, popularia carmina singing,
Happy with ale omnes – exceptis excipiendis.
Gloomily drives Jack Jones, inconsolabilis heros;
No companion habet, solus sine virgine coster.
Per Boro', per Fleet Street, per Strand, sic itur ad 'Empire';
Illinc Coventry Street peragunt in a merry procession,
Qua Piccadilly propinquat to Shaftesbury Avenue, tandem
Gloomily Jack vehitur.  Sed amet qui never amavit!
En! subito fugiunt dark thoughts; Arabella videtur.
Quum subit ullius pulcherrima bloomin' imago,
Corde juvat Jack Jones; exclamat loudly 'What oh, there!'
Maiden ait 'Deus, ecce deus!' floresque relinquit.
Post asinum sedet illa; petunt Welsh Harp prope Hendon.

O fons Brent Reservoir! recubans sub tegmine brolli,
Brachia complexus (yum, yum!) Jack kissed Arabella;
'Garn' ait illa rubens, et 'Garn' reboatur ab Echo;
Propositique tenax Jack 'Swelp me lummy, I loves yer.'
Hinc illae lacrimae: 'Jest one!' et 'Saucy, give over.'
Tempora jam mutantur, et hats; caligine cinctus
Oscula Jones iterat. mokoque immitit habenas.
Concertina manu sixteen discrimina vocum
Obliquitur; cantant (ne saevi, magne policeman)
Noctem in Old Kent Road.  Sic transit gloria Monday.

This macaronic poem is full of references to the classic authors which the reader is invited to identify (where they occur) from the main body of this work.

## Appendix II

### Motor Bus – A. D. Godley

What is this that roareth thus?
Can it be a Motor Bus?
Yes, the smell and hideous hum
Indicat Motorem Bum.
Implet in the Corn and High
Terror me Motoris Bi:
Bo Motori clamitabo
Ne Motore caedar a Bo –
Dative be or ablative
So thou only let us live:
Whither shall thy victims flee?
Spare us, spare us, Motor Be!
Thus I sang; and still anigh
Came in hordes Motores Bi,
Et complebat omne forum
Copia Motorum Borum.
How shall wretches live like us
Cincti Bis Motoribus?
Domine, defende nos
Contra hos Motores Bos!

The last four lines *anglice* read: "How shall wretches live like us surrounded by motor buses?  O Lord, defend us against these motor buses".

# Appendix III

**Abiit, excessit, evasit, erupit**
Cicero, *In Catilinam*, II, i. 1

**Ab ovo usque ad mala**
Horace, *Satires* I, iii. 6.

**Ars longa, vita brevis**
Seneca, *De Brevitate Vitae* (*Of the Brevity of Life*).

**Ave atque vale**
Catullus, *Carmina* ci. 10.

**Domus et placens uxor**
Horace, *Odes* II, xiv.

**Caelum non animum mutant qui trans mare currunt**
Horace, *Epistles*, I, xi. 27.

**Carpe diem**
Horace, *Odes*, I, xi. (the last line)

**Decus et tutamen (in armis)**
Virgil, *Aeneid*, v. 262

**Dulce est desipere in loco**
Horace, *Odes*, IV, xii. 28.

**Elegantiæ arbiter**
Tacitus, *Annals* xvi. sect. 18.

**E pluribus unus**
Virgil, *Moretum*, l04.

**Errare est humanum**
Seneca the Younger, *Naturales Quaestiones*, iv. ch. 2.

**Ex nihilo nihil fit**
Lucretius, *De Rerum Natura*, i. 155.

**Facilis descensus Averno;**
> **Noctes atque dies patet atri janua Ditis:**
> **Sed revocare gradum superasque evadere ad auras,**
> **Hoc opus, hic labor est.**
Virgil, *Aeneid*, vi. 126

**Favete linguis**
Horace, *Odes*, III, i. 2

**Felix qui potuit rerum cognoscere causas**
Virgil, *Georgics*, ii. 490

**Humanum est errare**
Seneca the Younger, *Naturales Quaestiones*, iv. ch. 2

**Indignor quandoque bonus dormitat Homerus**
Horace, *Ars Poetica* 359.

**In medias res**
Horace, *Ars Poetica*, 148

**Matre pulchra filia pulchrior**
Horace, *Odes* I, xvi.

**Maxima debetur puero reverentia**
Juvenal, *Satires* xiv. 47.

**Medio de fonte leporum surgit amari aliquid quod in ipsis floribus angat**
Lucretius, *De Rerum Natura*, iv. 1133.

**Mutato nomine de te fabula narratur**
Horace, *Satires* I, i. 69.

**Nescit vox missa reverti**
Horace, *Ars Poetica* 390.

**Ne sit ancillæ tibi amor pudori**
Horace, *Odes*, II, iv. 1.

**Nil posse creari de nilo**
Lucretius, *De Rerum Natura*, i. 155.

**Non compos mentis**
Cicero, *In Pisonem*, Ch.20, §48.

**Non omnis moriar**
Horace, *Odes*, III, xxx. 6

**Nunc est bibendum**
Horace, *Odes,* I xxxvii. 1.

**O Dea certe**
Virgil, *Aeneid*, i. 327

**Odi profanum vulgus et arceo**
Horace, *Odes*, III, i. 1.

**O mihi praeteritos referat si Iuppiter annos**
Virgil, *Aeneid*, viii. 560:

**Orandum est ut sit mens sana in corpore sano**
Juvenal, *Satires*, viii. 356.

**O tempora, o mores**
Cicero, *In Catalinam*, I, i. 1.

**Panem et circenses**
Juvenal, *Satires*, X, 81

**Parturient montes, nascetur ridiculus mus**
Horace, *Ars Poetica*, 139.

**Pede claudo**
Horace, *Odes*, III, ii. 32.

**Rara avis in terris, nigroque simillima cycno**
Juvenal, *Satires*, vi. 165.

**Sed fugit interea, fugit inreparabile tempus (Tempus fugit)**
Virgil, *Georgics*, iii. 284.

**Sic volo, sic jubeo**
Juvenal, *Satires*, vi. 223.

**Simplex munditiis**
Horace, *Odes* I, v, 5.

**Splendide mendax**
Horace, *Odes* III, xi.

**Sunt lacrimae rerum et mentem mortalia tangunt**
Virgil, *Aeneid*, i. 462.

**Ultima Thule**
Virgil, *Georgics*, I, 30.

**Video meliora proboque; deteriora sequor**
Ovid, *Metamorphoses*, vii. 20.

**Virginibus puerisque (canto)**
Horace, *Odes* III, i. 4,

**Virgo intacta**
Catullus, *Ode* 62, line 45.

**Vixi puellis nuper idoneus**
**Et militavi non sine gloria**
Horace, *Odes*, III, xxvi. 1

## Appendix IV
A Quick Reference List

**Ab incunabulo** *From the cradle*

**Ab initio** *From the beginning, at the outset*

**Ab origine** *From the beginning, from the source*

**Ab ovo usque ad mala** *From the egg (or from the start) to the apples (the finish)*

**Acta non verba** *Deeds not words*

**Addenda** *Things which are to be added*

**Ad infinitum** *To infinity*

**Ad libitum (ad lib)** *At pleasure*

**Ad nauseam** *Until it makes you sick*

**Aegrotat** *He is ill*

**Afflavit Deus et dissipantur** *God breathed and they are scattered*

**Alea iacta est** *The die is cast*

**Alias (dictus)** *At another time (under a different name)*

**Aliquando bonus dormitat Homerus** *Even good Homer nods at times*

**Amantium irae amoris integratio est** *Lovers' quarrels are the renewal of love*

**Amari aliquid** *Something bitter*

**Apologia** *A vindication*

**A posteriori** *From events coming after*

**Apparatus** *Things prepared*

**Aqua pura** *Pure water*

**Arbiter elegantiarum** *A judge of matters of taste*

**Ars longa, vita brevis** *Art is long, life is short,* or *So long a time to learn the art, so short a time to live*

**Ave atque vale** *Hail and farewell*

**Benedictus benedicat** *May the Blessed One give a blessing*

**Beneficium accipere libertatem est vendere** *To accept a favour is to sell one's liberty*

**Bis peccare in bello non licet** *In war one may not blunder twice*

**Cacoethes scribendi** *An itch for writing*

**Caelum non animum mutant qui trans mare currunt** *They change their skies but not their souls who flee across the sea*

**Camera obscura** *A darkened room*

**Caput mortuum** *A dead head*

**Carpe diem** *Reap the harvest of the day*

**Casus belli** *A reason for war, for dispute*

**Caveat emptor** *Let the buyer beware*

**Cave canem** *Beware of the dog*

**Citius, Altius, Fortius** *Faster, higher, stronger*

**Coitus interruptus** *Interrupted intercourse*

**Coitus plenus et optabilis** *Perfect and desirable coitus*

**Compos mentis** *Of sound mind*

**Consummatum est** *It is finished*

**Coram populo** *Before people, in public*

**Cornucopia** *The "horn of plenty", a source of unlimited wealth*

**Cum grano salis** *With a pinch (of salt)*

**Cum omnibus suis pertinenciis** *With all its appurtenances*

**Decus et tutamen (in armis)** *A beauteous safeguard (in battle)*

**De gustibus non est disputandum** *There is no arguing about taste*

**Delenda est Carthago** *Carthage must be destroyed*

**Denarius** *Penny*

**De novo** *Anew, from scratch*

**De profundis** *Out of the depths*

**Desiderata** *Things to be desired*

**Detur digniori** *Let it be given to the more deserving*

**Dies irae, dies illa, . . .** *That day is a day of wrath, . . .*

**Disjecta membra** *Dismembered limbs*

**Domus et placens uxor** *A home and a pleasing wife, a sweet wife*

**Dulce domum** *Sweet (is the sound of) home*

**Dulce est desipere in loco** *It is pleasant to let one's hair down on* *the right occasions*

**Elixir vitae**  *The elixir of life*

**E pluribus unum**  *From many [comes] the one*

**Errare est humanum**  *It is human to err*

**Est modus in rebus**  *There is a measure (or mean or middle course) in everything*

**Et in Arcadia ego**  *I too [have lived] in Arcadia*

**Ex Africa semper aliquid novi**  *There is always something new out of Africa*

**Excelsior**  *Higher*

**Exceptis excipiendis**  *With proper exceptions*

**Exeunt omnes**  *They (all) go out*

**Ex gratia**  *By kindness*

**Ex nihilo nihil fit**  *Nothing comes of nothing*

**Ex voto**  *In consequence of a vow*

**Facilis descensus Averno**  *The descent to Avernus is easy*

**Facsimile**  *Make the same*

**Fatigatus et aegrotus**  *Tired and sick*

**Fauna**  *Wildlife*

**Favete linguis**  *Be favourable to your tongues*

**Feliciter audax**  *Happily daring*

**Felix qui potuit (rerum cognoscere causas)**  *Happy is he who has been able (to find out the causes of things)*

**Ferae naturae**  *Of a wild nature*

**Festina lente**  *Hasten slowly*

**Fiat**  *Let it be*

**Fiat lux**  *Let there be light*

**Flora**  *The goddess of flowers*

**Fons et origo**  *The source and origin*

**Fragrat post funera virtus**  *Virtue smells sweet after death*

**Gaudeamus igitur, juvenes dum sumus**  *Let us rejoice therefore, while we are still young*

**Gratias tibi agimus** *We give thee thanks*

**Habeas corpus** *You have the body*

**Hic haec hoc** *This, this, this*

**Hinc illae lacrimae** *Hence those tears*

**Impedimenta** *Encumbrances, impediments*

**In absentia** *In one's absence*

**In articulo mortis** *At the point of death, in the arms of death*

**In flagrante delicto** *In the act*

**In loco parentis** *In place of a parent*

**In medias res** *Into the thick of things*

**In situ** *In place*

**In statu pupillari** *In the position of a ward*

**Integer vitae scelerisque purus** *(He who is) blameless in respect to his life, and has no share in wickedness (need not carry spears, poisoned arrows, etc)*

**In toto** *In total, altogether*

**In transitu** *In transit*

**In vacuo** *In a vacuum*

**In vinculis matrimonii** *In the bonds of marriage*

**Ius primae noctis** *The right of the first night*

**Laborare est orare (*or* orare est laborare)** *To work is to pray (*or *work is prayer)*

**Lapsus linguae** *A slip of the tongue*

**Lares et penates** *Household gods*

**Latet anguis in herba** *A snake lurks in the grass*

**Locus classicus** *The stock example, the classic example*

**Locus standi** *A place for standing, a right to interfere*

**Loquitur** *Speaks*

**Lustrum** *A period of five years*

**Lusus naturae** *A freak of nature*

**Mare nostrum** *Our sea*

**Matre pulchra filia pulchrior** *Fairer daughter of a fair mother*

**Maxima debetur puero reverentia** *The utmost reverence is due to a child*

**Mea culpa** *Through my fault*

**Media vita in morte sumus** *In the midst of life we are in death*

**Memento** *A keepsake, a reminder*

**Mirabile dictu** *Wonderful to relate*

**Mobile perpetuum** *Perpetual motion*

**Modus operandi (M.O.)** *The way of working*

**Modus vivendi** *A way of living (together)*

**Mons Veneris** *The Mount of Venus*

**Multum in parvo** *Much in a small space*

**Mutatis mutandis** *With the necessary changes being made*

**Mutato nomine de te fabula narratur** *Change the name and the story applies to yourself*

**Nemo me impune lacessit** *No one provokes me with impunity*

**Ne plus ultra** *No more, no further, the ultimate*

**Nescit vox missa reverti** *The published word can never be recalled*

**Ne sit ancillæ tibi amor pudori** *Do not be ashamed of your love for a serving-maid*

**Nil volva pulchrius ampla** *Nothing more beautiful than a sizeable volva*

**Noctes ambrosianæ** *Ambrosian nights, delightful nights*

**Noli me tangere** *Touch me not*

**Non compos mentis** *Not of sound mind, mentally challenged*

**Non est inventus** *He cannot be found*

**Non omnis moriar** *I shall not wholly die*

**Non sequitur** *It does not follow*

**Nunc est bibendum** *Now is the time to drink*

**Nunquam ubi sub ubi** *Never where under where*

**O Dea certe** *O Goddess beyond doubt!*

**Odi profanum vulgus et arceo** *I hate the common herd and steer clear of them*

**O mihi praeteritos referat si Iuppiter annos** *If only Jupiter would restore to me the years (that are) fled*

**Omnibus** *For all*

**Omnium gatherum** *A comprehensive collection*

**Orandum est ut sit mens sana in corpore sano** *You must pray for a sound mind in a sound body*

**O tempora, o mores** *O what times! O what conduct!*

**Pabulum** *Food, fodder*

**Panem et** circenses *Bread and circuses*

**Panis angelicus** *Angelic bread, the bread of angels*

**Pari passu** *With equal pace, together*

**Parturiunt montes nascetur ridiculus mus** *The mountains labour and shall spawn a laughable little mouse*

**Pede claudo** *With halting foot*

**Per ardua ad astra** *Through toil to the stars*

**Perpetuum mobile** *Perpetual motion*

**Per se** *On its own, by itself*

**Persona non grata** *An unacceptable person*

**Pervigilium Veneris** *The Eve of Venus*

**Placentae angelicae** *Angel cakes*

**Post coitum triste** *After coitus (one is) sad*

**Post hoc, ergo propter hoc** *After this, therefore because of this*

**Post mortem** *After death*

**Praemonitus, praemunitus** *Forewarned is forearmed*

**Proxime accessit** *Came (close) second*

**Pudenda** *Things to be ashamed of*

**Quam celerrime** *As quickly as possible*

**Quid pro quo** *Something equivalent in return*

**Quota** *A share*

**Quo vadis?** *Whither goest thou?*

**Rara avis (in terris, nigroque simillima cycno)** *A rare bird (on earth, like a black swan)*

**Requiescat in pace (R.I.P.)** *May he/she rest in peace*

**Resurgam**  *I shall rise again*

**Rigor mortis**  *A stiffening of the body in death*

**Sic volo, sic jubeo**  *Such is my will, such is my command*

**Simplex munditiis**  *Simple in (your/his/her/their) elegance*

**Sine nomine**  *Without a name*

**Sine qua non**  *Without which nothing*

**Siste, viator**  *Pause, traveller*

**Si vis pacem, para bellum**  *If you want peace, prepare for war*

**Solvitur ambulando**  *It is solved by walking*

**Splendide mendax**  *Splendidly false, or Nobly untruthful*

**Status quo (ante)**  *Previous state, situation*

**Stella maris**  *Star of the sea*

**Stet**  *Let it stand*

**Sine nomine**  *Without a name*

**Sui generis**  *Of its own kind, "one of a kind"*

**Sunt lacrimae rerum et mentem mortalia tangunt**  *Tears abound in all things and human suffering touches the heart*

**Supera moras**  *Overcome delays*

**Suum cuique bene olet**  *What is one's own smells sweet*

**Tabula rasa**  *A clean slate*

**Taedium vitae**  *Boredom, the tedium of living*

**Tandem**  *At length*

**Tempus edax rerum**  *Time the devourer of things*

**Tempus fugit**  *Time flies (or flees)*

**Terra incognita**  *The Unknown Land*

**Tertium quid**  *A third something*

**Timor mortis conturbat me**  *The fear of death disturbs me*

**Tityre, tu patulae recubans sub tegmine fagi**  *Tityrus, thou lying canopied beneath thy spreading beech-tree*

**Totis viribus**  *With all (my) strength*

**Trivia**  *Trifles*

**Ultima Thule**  *Farthest Thule*

**Ultra vires**  *Beyond one's powers*

**Vade mecum**  *Go with me*

**Veni, vidi, vici**  *I came, I saw, I conquered*

**Via Dolorosa**  *The Way of Sorrows*

**Video meliora proboque; deteriora sequor**  *I see and approve the better (path), but follow the worse*

**Virginibus puerisque (canto)**  *To maidens and young men (I sing)*

**Virgo intacta**  *A virgin*

**Vis inertiae**  *The power of inertia, of inactivity*

**Vis medicatrix naturae**  *The healing power of Nature*

**Vixi puellis nuper idoneus**  *In those days I lived equipped for ladies' love*

**Vox et praeterea nihil**  *A voice and nothing more*

## Postscript

Wherever we go in our journey through the intricate paths of the English language, we cannot escape the influence of Latin. Latin has long been a linguistic meadow from which innovative writers throughout the centuries have culled the blossoms they needed to put their burgeoning thoughts into words, and the identification of these writers and the chronology of their inventions and borrowings is a fascinating study.

We meet Latin more directly in the scientific names which have been given to living creatures, a subject which requires a book (or books) to itself. Each creature has a generic or general name, identifying its *genus*, followed by a specific or special name, identifying its *species*. Some names are classical Latin. *Bufo* was Latin for "a toad" and the scientific name for a common toad is *Bufo bufo*, a rare case of the two names being identical. (Another case is the wren, *Troglodytes troglodytes*.) The natterjack toad, *Bufo calamita*, is also a toad of the *bufo* genus, but of a different species. Its name might be thought to suggest some connection with ill-luck, but *calamita* was the name given by the Romans to a small green frog who lived among reeds (*calami*). (*Calamus* was also the name given to a pen made from a reed – cf. *lapsus calami* in the main body of this book *s.v lapsus linguae.*) A sparrow in Latin was *passer*, and the house sparrow is *Passer domesticus*, while the Spanish sparrow is *Passer hispaniolensis*.

(Confusingly, the *Puffinus puffinus* is not the puffin, but the Manx shearwater. The puffin is *Fratercula arctica*. *"Fraterculus"* is Latin for "little brother", but the ending –*a* is a feminine ending, and so technically the puffin is the "little feminine brother of the Arctic regions".)

Naturally the Romans had names for those plants and creatures with which they were familiar. In Latin *rana* was "frog" and *ranunculus* was "little frog", but the latter name was also given to the crowfoot plant, so the water crowfoot is *Ranunculus aquitilis* and the ivy-leaved crowfoot is *Ranunculus hederaceus*. The crowfoot was of the same genus as the buttercup, and so the common meadow buttercup is *Ranunculus acris* ("the acrid little frog") while *Ranunculus repens* is the creeping buttercup. Much can be gleaned from the specific name about the habit or qualities of the plant or animal. *Pratensis* indicates that a plant's habitat is meadows, while *officinalis* indicates that it has medical uses. *Repens* and *reptans* both mark its habit of regenerating itself by "creeping" and putting down fresh roots at intervals. From the verb *reptare* comes the word *reptilia* which the Authorised Version translates correctly and all-inclusively in Genesis i. 24 as "creeping things". Modern versions of the Bible choose to translate *reptilia* as "reptiles", thereby rather unkindly excluding ants, butterflies, spiders, scorpions, millipedes *et alia* from the creation myth.

These ancient names were not enough to go around when Linnæus and others began their great task of assigning scientific names. The use of much imagination was clearly called for. Many plants have Greek generic names with Latin specific names, so *Cephalanthera rubra* is the red helleborine, a red (*rubra*) flower whose anther (*anthera*) looks very like a head (*kephale*). Others have Greek names or Greek forms of names for both genus and species: for example the corky-fruited water dropwort is *Œnanthe pimpinelloides,* the "wine-flower" with a resemblance to the pimpernel or burnet. This is indeed a field with rich etymological pickings.

While we are on the subject of Greek, it is worth looking at two of the very few Greek words or phrases which have been adopted by English speakers. The words "phenomenon" and "criterion" are singular in Greek and should so be in English. Their plurals are "phenomena" and "criteria" respectively and thus it is incorrect to speak, as a small number of people do, of "a phenomena" or "a criteria".

Again, the phrase "hoi polloi" seems now to drop easily from the English-speaker's lips. In Greek "hoi" is "the" and "polloi" is "people", and "hoi polloi" are "the (common) people". It is unnecessary to speak of "*the* hoi polloi", which is "the the people". We are slowly being educated in Japanese to the extent that we talk of "Mount Fuji" or of simply "Fujiyama" rather than of "Mount Fujiyama", so the correct use of "hoi polloi" should not present too much of a challenge.

*Finis*